THE
GRACE
OF THE
ROSARY

THE GRACE OF THE ROSARY

Scripture, Contemplation, and the Claim of the Kingdom of God

DAVID P. REID

Paulist Press
New York/Mahwah, N.J.

IMPRIMI POTEST: Very Rev. Enrique Losada, SS.CC.
Superior General
September 11, 2005, Rome, Italy

Cover & book design by Sharyn Banks

Library of Congress Cataloging-in-Publication Data

Reid, David P.
    The grace of the rosary : Scripture, contemplation, and the claim of the kingdom of God / David P. Reid.
        p. cm.
    Includes bibliographical references.
    ISBN 0-8091-4427-1 (alk. paper)
1. Spiritual life—Catholic Church. 2. Rosary. I. Title.
    BX2350.3.R45   2006
    242'.74—dc22   2006019568

Published by Paulist Press
997 Macarthur Boulevard
Mahwah, New Jersey 07430

www.paulistpress.com

Printed and bound in the
United States of America

CONTENTS

Contents

PREFACE

In connecting the two sides of my life, academia and pastoral service, I am always searching for the bridge between our faith and how we practice it. For many the Rosary is such a bridge. As a tool of contemplation, praying the Rosary invites one to place the template of our lived experience alongside the template of the gospel story. When I read the letter of John Paul II on the Rosary, not only his reflection on contemplation spoke to me, but also the understanding that the Rosary could be seen as a way to own the claim of the kingdom, a claim that ultimately cries out for a world shaped by social justice. The Rosary is no flight from the world but a way to engage challenges from an experience of Christ, broken down bite-size into the mysteries of Jesus' life, death, and resurrection. The Rosary, as the pope says, is basically centered on Christ, and we are led to contemplate Christ and his meaning for our lives today by no less a skilled contemplative than Mary.

At the end of text is a study guide with questions for the introduction and four chapters. These questions may be used for either personal reflection or for a parish course in continuing education. I have also added in an appendix a grid of the twenty mysteries. The grid may be read vertically to give us the mysteries in the order I have presented them, beginning with the new Mysteries of Light. The horizontal reading reveals a pattern of *claim* (Luminous), *counter-claim* (Sorrowful), *acclaim* (Glorious), and *proclaim* (Joyful). This particular arrangement, leading to the One Mystery who is the Christ of God, helps greatly in retreats I offer on the mysteries of the Rosary. The grid may, in fact, also function as a good way to summarize, in a sixth session, a parish course.

ACKNOWLEDGMENTS

How much I have depended on others in offering this work on the Rosary is evident. I am as grateful to the many with whom I have worked pastorally as to the many from whom I have learned at the Washington Theological Union, St. Bernard's Institute (Rochester, New York), and elsewhere. I acknowledge with gratitude these living sources. I dedicate the work to the members of the Congregation, and I thank the dedicated professional staff on this the centennial of our arrival in Fairhaven, 1905. All biblical quotations are taken with gratitude from the New Revised Standard Version.

INTRODUCTION

NEW INSIGHTS
FROM A NEW ARRANGEMENT

A friend reminded me recently of how often I referred to going as a youth to the shrine of Mary at Knock, County Mayo, Ireland. When I was growing up in Dublin, my family would travel some 260 miles, round trip, to Knock about three times a year, with fifteen mysteries of the Rosary on the way and the same on the return journey. My friend's comment came when I was experiencing the grace to return to an earlier practice in my life—that of praying the Rosary on journeys.

That return had its own beginning when I took over a car previously driven by a confrere. I received his car when he died. I was happy with his car but more intrigued by the set of large rosary beads that he kept close to hand. Why, I do not know, but one day, I picked up the beads and I prayed the Rosary. This was a turning point, a graced moment, because for many years I had not done so.

I believe firmly that one needs to discern the call of the Spirit to engage in any popular devotion, be it the Rosary, the Stations of the Cross, a novena to a saint, or First Fridays. While I believe in the necessity of such devotions and think that our Catholic life is bereft when they fall away, I also believe that the practice of any devotion needs to be discerned. Whenever people asked me *why*

1

I did not pray the Rosary, I said, "It is not my grace." A "not my grace" approach to the practice of popular devotion opens one up to the freedom to know one's own likes and dislikes, one's own inspirations and enthusiasm; then, when the time of grace does come, the freedom to say "yes" freely. The Jesuit publication *America* ran a series of articles on popular devotions during Lent of 2003.[1] In following the series, I learned that others had similar experiences. I have no regrets. I do indeed have gratitude that a practice from my earlier life returned with a new impulse and relevance.

Thus the late John Paul II's *Rosarium Virginis Mariae* (herein *RVM*), his 2002 letter on the Rosary, was particularly compelling to me, as we will see often over the course of these pages.[2] What drew me in was his way of interfacing Jesus and Mary. I use the word *interfacing* advisedly because John Paul refers often to the face of Jesus, both in this writing and in earlier encyclicals. John Paul contemplates Mary beholding the face of Jesus. The contemplation of the contemplation by Mary of the face of Jesus draws me close to the heart-to-heart relationship between Jesus and Mary that is central to the spirituality of the Congregation of the Sacred Hearts of Jesus and Mary to which I belong. John Paul writes (*RVM*, nos. 10, 2, and 15, respectively):

> The eyes of her heart already turned to him at the Annunciation, when she conceived him by the power of the Holy Spirit....The mysteries of the Rosary put us in living communion with Jesus through the heart of his mother....Never as in the Rosary do the life of Jesus and that of Mary appear so deeply joined. Mary lives only in Christ and for Christ.

About the time I was returning to the Rosary, as a good expression of my community's spirituality, I rediscovered my earlier fascination with the *Pietà* of Michelangelo as expressive of Mary's lineage in Judaic spirituality. One could say that religious art is like a bridge to the Rosary that developed over centuries. The prayer form of the mysteries blossomed from contemplation of artistic scenes from the life of Christ, knitted together with *Aves* whose very number recalled the 150 psalms of Israel.[3] Michelangelo surely combines face-to-face, heart-to-heart dimensions of the mother and son. As Jesus' body grows cold and stiffens on her lap, I envision Mary as crushed and forlorn in losing Jesus. Yet, she is confident and hopeful in the depth of her faith that he is that servant of God who will not be abandoned, the stone rejected that will become the cornerstone.

Where else would Mary turn in her anguish than to the psalms, the key expressions of Judaism's spirituality? The face-to-face, heart-to-heart relationship of Jesus and Mary is embedded in their shared Judaic spirituality of profound and radical trust in the fidelity of God to God's promises. Mary's deepest strength at her worst moment was her belief that God would be faithful. God makes and keeps promises, and that is the basis of God's claim upon Mary and upon us. In recalling the events of Jesus' life, death, and resurrection—called mysteries—the Rosary celebrates promises made and promises fulfilled. A mystery is a secret disclosed in God's way and freedom, a source of endless contemplation. Pope John Paul entitled one section of his letter on the Rosary, "From 'mysteries' to the Mystery: Mary's way."

With the grace to return to the Rosary, I could see more clearly than before that the Rosary is a constellation of mysteries. I relate with the words used by Paul VI in *Marialis Cultus* (1974)

3

and borrowed by John Paul in the second paragraph of his own letter: "a compendium of the gospel." What becomes apparent in the practice of praying the Rosary is that this summing up is not an external, mechanical imposition of prescribed thoughts and images on a substratum of two hundred Hail Marys. There is an internal coherence to *all* the mysteries in the one Mystery. Once the Christian praying the Rosary is given the grace to approach the one Mystery, then the ebb and flow of the mysteries lift the person and carry him or her along with the unfolding of the plan of God for our salvation. Problems are to be solved, but mysteries are to be lived. Mystery is never exhausted. So a person is touched by mystery in the many mysteries of the Rosary. These are none other than the Mysteries of our Christian creed, the *mirabilia Dei*, the wonderful deeds of God. The person finds himself or herself engulfed in the richness of the Mystery of God in Christ. John Paul turns to the Letter to the Ephesians to find language, albeit barely adequate, to express this fullness. He cites Ephesians 3:17–19, noting the author's heartfelt prayer[4]

> that Christ may dwell in your hearts through faith, as you are being rooted and grounded in love. I pray that you may have the power to comprehend, with all the saints, what is the breadth and length and height and depth, and to know the love of Christ that surpasses knowledge, so that you may be filled with all the fullness of God.

One cultural phenomenon I noticed when I returned to praying the Rosary is that Rosary beads are used more often today as a piece of jewelry. Wearing the beads like this appears to be a misuse for they are not an amulet, nor do they carry power within themselves. Praying the Rosary is not a form of magic. However, one needs to slow down on being judgmental on this point. It could be that when teenagers wear the beads around their neck, they are indeed making a statement, an assurance that someone, perhaps a grandmother at home, is praying the Rosary for their protection.

My return to the Rosary is a step forward in a search to bring the findings of modern biblical study to bear on the life of each Catholic Christian. My goal is to promote a biblical spirituality. By spirituality I mean a making of one's own the mysteries of our religion, an absorption in story, symbol, and practice of the tenets of the Nicene or Apostles' Creed, transforming our identity. Spirituality is saying "yes" to the truths of our faith in a way that gives substance and shapes the interiority of our lives. Call this process a "holistic appropriation" if you will. By this I mean a making one's own of the faith that reaches way beyond the head into the heart, the feelings, into the way one views one's world that touches affectively every relationship that we have and that we are. Without connecting all these components of our human existence, how can anyone make heads or tails of life in this world today? There needs to be a coherence between life lived on the outside—what we *do* and *say*—and the life we live on the inside—what we *think* and *feel*. Who can sustain the overload of any one day in our modern world of heightened stimulation unless he or she is building an interior scaffolding of symbol and meaning? Over against the eminent threat of overwhelming alienation and isolation, we need a world of shared values, symbols, and practices of belonging and inclusion. The Christian religion supplies us with such integration if we have assimilated an underlying story that paradoxically binds and liberates in a covenantal relationship with others.

Biblical spirituality is the construction of such a world of meaning. To be sure, the Bible is itself a world of immense diversity. But where is the unity, where is the one symbol that holds it all together? A biblical spirituality can emerge from a process of absorbing the truthfulness of the Bible in a way that both unifies the biblical message and gives to the believing community a compelling grasp of what God is saying to us in the midst of our earthly journey. One does not come to such a grasp of his or her faith in a matter of days—not even in a matter of years. The development of a spirituality is a lifelong undertaking, but some central beams appear early. One person will name "covenant" such a key vortex, another will name the "awesomeness of God," another will marvel at the earthiness of divine revelation, and another will be absorbed by the image of God as speaker of the word.

One concern of modern biblical scholarship is to provide a grasp of the Bible that will promote this holistic, affective appropriation. This is not the place to tell the fascinating history of the modern study of the Bible, reaching back to Richard Simon in the mid-1600s.[5] It *is* the place, though, to rejoice that the fruit of that history has been to give the modern church a table full of rich food for liturgy, spirituality, and theological reflection, as noted in the declaration on the renewal of the liturgy at Vatican II.[6] The church has never been without the Bible, without an affective appropriation of its truth. What's new is the democratization of the use of the Bible. As individual persons, we have the Bible in our own hands, able to read it and appreciate it as the religious literature of a community of faith with whom we are connected in the marvelous continuity of God's love, a connection that we bring to bear on every aspect of our lives and that we express in liturgy. The faith convictions of the Bible are embedded in an astounding display of literary forms, and we are constantly teased into active imaging of the ways that God as creator and redeemer communicates to us. The encyclical of Pius XII *Divino Afflante Spiritu* (1943) and the document on revelation from Vatican II (1964), *Dei Verbum,* are watershed moments in the history of biblical study. They appreciate the phenomenon of the Bible as the necessary literary component in the development of the Judeo-Christian movement.

In terms of biblical spirituality, literature should be broadly understood to embrace not only written material but also the oral traditions that a community has cultivated long before anything is set down in writing. Thus, literature is a way that a people sets down its tradition. Writing is often not only a follow-up on the development of the tradition but a way to hold onto the tradition and transmit it from one generation to another, from one locale to another. The study of all the changes that happen as traditions are handed on is a huge field of study, but it is never distant from our lives. We hand on traditions every day in how we take our experiences and put them into a story in order to tell a friend, write home to family and add to the community lore. No sooner have we experienced something than we are already translating it into words and images and investing those words and images with stirred-up emotions.

Modern biblical scholarship respects profoundly this storytelling aspect of human living and claims that the story of the Bible is released to the reader who brings to the text his or her own way of traditioning life's experiences. Given wider aspects and different ways to view circumstances—for example, through the healing of memories—a person's own story can be transformed. Similarly, the collected traditions of the Bible are heard in the context of experiencing God as faithful to a covenantal relationship in the ups and downs of historical experience. The question "What do *I* bring to the story?" is as critical as the question "What do I get out of it?" I hope this reflection thus far persuades you that biblical spirituality is a demandingly interactive, participative, and affective appropriation that comes as the fruits of not only opening the Bible but personal involvement with the story it tells. The text of the Bible is porous; it is a medium through which we encounter the presence of God speaking to us. We are involved in fashioning our own story from it and in discovering parts of our own story yet unopened to us.

Biblical scholars ask a series of questions: Where is the word of God—in the text, in the hearer, in the speaking of God? Where is revelation? Is revelation contained somewhere?[7] Is revelation a thing contained or an action joining two subjects? Is the Bible the container of revealed truths or the mediation of a self-revealing, truthful God? The emphasis is put on the experience of God presently revealing Godself to us, and the text is the mediation between God revealing and God's people hearing. In this sense the Bible is most at home in the liturgical assembly when the lector says at the end of the reading "the word of the Lord."[8] The tradition lives on because the traditioning process is alive!

In this understanding of tradition, the most important question that one can ask is this: Why did the people of the Bible tell the story this way? This question may yield more than the question What happened?[9] For example, the question for a person reading the passion of Jesus is less what happened and more why: Why do the evangelists present it in the way that they do? This is even more exciting when each evangelist writes differently about the same event. These questions enable the art of dialoguing with the text. By "dialogue," I mean bringing to bear on the text our varied experiences of the one God whose love is fresh for every generation of readers, and for every moment in the historical unfolding of the riches of creation. The text no longer divides subject and object but is the ground between two subjects, communities over the course of great distances and great shifts in time and perspective but sharing the same faith. "Why did they tell the story this way?" This way the dialogue with the community telling the story is ever-sharpened and indeed the mediator of a revealing God.

This dialogue leads to contemplation. In his letter on the Rosary, John Paul devotes much attention to the question of contemplation.[10] The word itself is deserving of sustained reflection. From the Latin *templum,* meaning "space marked out for observation of auguries" *(Webster's Collegiate),* the word introduces the idea of observing divinations, actions thought to be of divine origin. The word *template,* with which we have become very familiar by way of computer and engineering sciences, means a gauge, pattern, or mold used as a guide. Its concrete use is, however, also enlightening: "a short piece placed horizontally in a wall under a beam to distribute its weight or pressure, as over a door or window frame."

Certainly the practice of contemplation can carry, to great advantage, all these significances. "To template alongside with"—the literal meaning of *contemplate*—indicates a process of building analogies and correspondences, and discovering certain duality, mutuality, and even reciprocity. The process of making events available to our consciousness through literature is contemplation in this very literal sense. Templates are laid alongside each other, the template of our human experience and the template of faith. Templates distribute weight over the door of life! To put into word, symbol, and drama the experience of Jesus, each mystery is templated by the early Christian community in each life situation.

Therefore, the first question to pose is, Why did the Christian community choose to hand on the story in this way? And another question is, What do *we* bring to the unfolding of the mystery? In choosing these two questions, we are applying our own template. The world created by the templates of the early Christian community meets the world templated by the modern listening, praying, reflecting, and reading community. While the word *mystery* often suggests wanting to hide its contents, it can connote disclosure, never brought to the point of exhaustion! Inexhaustible and mystery seem to be twined! The contemplation of mysteries involves a process of inexhaustible enrichment, a desire to make oneself known and a corresponding desire to know more of the other communicant.

John Paul, mystic that he was, connected contemplation to the experience of glory, a metaphor most apt to explore and enrich the experience that underlies the action of contemplation. Glory denotes the gravitas, the weightiness, the majesty, the beauty of the one beheld, but also includes the affect—the feelings and emotions—of the one beholding. To glory in your child's victory on the sports field is to enter into that victory or display of skill and art and to be transformed by the experience. The experience always yields transformation! John Paul makes his own the apostle Paul's description in 2 Corinthians 3:18 "And all of us, with unveiled faces, seeing the glory of the Lord as though reflected in a mirror, are being transformed into the same image from one degree of glory to another; for this comes from the Lord, the Spirit."[11]

The Apostle Paul describes what I meant earlier in saying that spirituality is making one's own the message of the gospel. Contemplation is a means of that affective appropriation of the glory in the gospel experience. This effectively means that contemplation is not merely a cerebral action but a holistic personal engagement, even fascination, with the One beheld in glory. The pope captured this affectiveness in the discussion of Mary as model of contemplation. He introduced the Hebrew word *zakar*, meaning "a making present of the works brought about by God in the history of salvation."[12] The transformative power of the experience arises from the fact that God remembers and never forgets. In turn, we remember because God never fails us, never forgets. Our memory functions within the acknowledgment of God as personally involved in God's own self-revelation to us for our salvation. This gives Mary a unique gift of discernment, which itself is a gift of the Spirit: "He has helped his servant Israel, / in remembrance of his mercy, / according to the promise he made to our ancestors" (Luke 1:54).

In adding ideas of glory and remembrance to the discussion of the contemplation of Mystery, we explore the graciousness of God's relationship with us. God's word carries God's own energy into the contemplative action. Mystery is transformative. The template of God calls forth the template of our human existence. While the template of our human experience is integral to the experience, it appears out of the fog of our human journeying, summoned by the template of God's actions on our behalf in the ongoing history of our salvation. Note John's words in the beginning of his Gospel, "grace upon grace" (1:16), and Paul's use of the "how much more surely"—or in today's diction, "how much the more"—as a principle of interpretation (v. 15 in Rom 5:12–21). The process of transformation is from grace to grace, glory to glory. If we would not know sin unless we experienced grace, how much more will we experience grace out of the experience of grace! Whether our mystery is one of grace or one of the struggle with evil, God's side of the contemplation is always grace in abundance.

In speaking about evil, we are bordering on one of the more controversial ways to speak of contemplation. The template that we bring is shaped often by sin and the struggle to overcome temptation. The Rosary, as any liturgy or private devotion, is never intended to take place in a "no sin zone." In this world, we are who we are, misshaped by a long history of saying "no" to God. Even creation groans in looking for the fullness of redemption (Rom 8:22). In Matthew's Gospel, the death of Jesus precipitated an earthquake (27:51). Jesus' invitation in Gethsemane to watch one hour with him (Matt 26:41) is an invitation to contemplate the struggle of grace and disgrace—but, let me hasten to add, only from the side of the victory of Jesus Christ in his death and resurrection. The Rosary is the contemplation, out of the depth of our need for forgiveness and liberation, of the mysteries of God's story with us in redemption and creation. To contemplate, therefore, has a profoundly missionary dimension. Is it a total surprise then that the contemplative Thérèse of Lisieux is the copatroness of the missions?

John Paul II in *Rosarium Virginis Mariae* considered this reality of sinfulness all too briefly. Yet it is in praying the Rosary that so many people have been able to take the story that crystallizes in the liturgy of the death and resurrection and apply it to the battles in their personal lives. The contemplation that is the heart of the experience of praying the Rosary helps many people to bring the victory of God's love and grace to bear down on the struggle against many countervailing forces released into our world by greed, exploitation, and deception. The Rosary, like any other form of Christian contemplation, is not a flight from the world but an embrace of the Risen Lord in the midst of the struggle that shows up on kitchen tables throughout the world. For many, the Rosary is taking the victory celebrated in the liturgy and giving it "real time" in their own human lives. There is not a mystery in the present praying of the Rosary that does not evoke an image of the conflict that goes on daily in our human lives. John Paul asks: "How could one possibly contemplate the mystery of the child of Bethlehem...without expressing the desire to welcome, defend, and promote life and to shoulder the burden of suffering children all over the world?"[13] Many similar questions will come to the fore as we examine in detail each mystery of the Rosary. Today, thanks to modern telecommunications, we are immensely aware of the enormity of the mystery of iniquity (see 2 Thess 2:7), ranging from the exploitation of workers, abuse of children, systematic torture, and institutionalized greed, to the constant abuse of the second commandment by churches claiming God's authority but acting contrary to the divine plan.

Thus, a full praying of the Rosary takes its place in the midst of an active practice of living out what is now called Catholic social teaching, formulated in great detail in a body of social teaching introduced by Leo XIII (who, incidentally, is heralded as the great pope of the Rosary). Paul VI, who called the work of justice a constitutive part of the proclamation of the gospel, combined a passion for justice with a strong Marian devotion. John Paul II likewise saw the Rosary as part of the new evangelization, a proclamation of the Gospel within the structures of the real world. One cannot for long interface the template of modern life with its joys and sorrows with the template of the saving mysteries of God without wanting to be part of the solution. The authenticity of any expression of Christian faith is discerned in how a Christian lives out, in the relationships and daily routines of his or her life, these dramatic claims of God's kingdom upon us. Thus a thirst for social justice can emerge from a healthy contemplation provoked by a no-holds-barred praying of the Rosary.[14]

This brings us to the powerful addition to the Rosary suggested by John Paul, but also some critical comments about the addition. The pope speaks of an addition that broadens the traditional pattern "to include the mysteries of Christ's ministry between his baptism and his passion."[15] In his public ministry, the mystery of Christ is most evidently a mystery of light: "As long as I am in the world, I am the light of the world" (John 9:5). The five significant moments during this phase of Christ's life are "(1) his Baptism in the Jordan; (2) his self-manifestation at the wedding of Cana; (3) his proclamation of the Kingdom of God, with his call to conversion; (4) his transfiguration; and finally, (5) his institution of the Eucharist as the sacramental expression of the Paschal Mystery."[16] The addition of the Mysteries of Light is a powerful reanchoring of the Rosary in the life and ministry of Jesus of Nazareth. Up to now, the Sorrowful Mysteries appeared without an introduction in the ministry of Jesus; whereas for the evangelists, the presentation of the events of the final week is deeply shaped by the previous presentation of his life and ministry.

The center mystery in the new five is the proclamation of the kingdom of God with the call to conversion. This proclamation is presented in the New Testament not as a singular event, but as the overall metaphor for the life and ministry of Jesus. In the building-of-the-kingdom metaphor, Jesus engaged the whole person in his and her many social dimensions. Sometimes, our emphasis in presenting the kingdom is too cerebral, with an emphasis on teaching that leads to moral conversion. While authentic, this is but one aspect of the New Testament presentation. Were the miracles and parables *only* teaching would they have engaged the disciples of Jesus in envisioning a different way of being in the world? The kingdom is primarily an experience of power, or better said, an experience of being empowered for life in the here and now. As we will see, *this* understanding of the kingdom lends itself well to grasping the metaphor of the kingdom as what holds all the other mysteries of the Rosary together. If a mystery is anything, it is boundless. One mystery bleeds into the other. Moreover, is not the recognition of permeable boundaries key to the art of contemplation?

The final Mystery of Light, the institution of the Eucharist as the sacramental expression of the paschal mystery, is marvelously placed as the intense culmination of the life and ministry of Jesus.[17] The entire ministry of Jesus, shaped as it was by table-companionship, pivots around the story of the Last Supper, clearly reflecting a conviction common to all the evangelists; however, the word *institute* used to introduce the mystery may be too influenced by later theology. The use of such formal words leads one to wonder whose structures are at play here, structures proper to the gospel unfolding of who Jesus is, or structures—and therefore concerns and problems—of a later age.

The insertion of the new mysteries between the Joyful and the Sorrowful Mysteries raises a similar consideration. I believe that the new Mysteries of Light aptly precede the Sorrowful, especially with the Last Supper scene immediately ahead of the mystery of Jesus' agony in the garden, but I do not think that they belong after the Joyful. While all the mysteries are postresurrection reflections on the life and ministry of Jesus of Nazareth, the Glorious and Joyful Mysteries are most evidently so.

My preference is to start with the Luminous Mysteries, beginning the ministry of Jesus with the baptism by John, then the Sorrowful Mysteries, culminating in the crucifixion. The Glorious Mysteries follow and bring us to Mary as the disciple who is presented as totally claimed by God in the reign of her son Jesus. From that vantage point of the glory of the Risen Lord, we then have the Joyful Mysteries that are a *rereading* of the whole of Jesus' life. Also, this rearrangement would honor the perspective of Luke from whom we draw all five Joyful Mysteries. This evangelist presents Mary singing an aria that gives us insight into how God works in all of God's relationships with us. Her Magnificat, as her canticle is more popularly known, reaches back into the past of God's promises to the ancestors and ahead to the future of the fulfillment of all promises. Likewise, the Joyful Mysteries, although presented in the domestic dimensions of home and family, are stories with a wide range of meanings. I suggest this order certainly for the private praying of the Rosary, maybe also for the public recitation since it is a devotional practice and, not being held to the rigors of public worship, can be freely adapted.[18]

My suggestions have the advantage of bringing us back into a consideration of what holds the Rosary together. Earlier, in discussing the third new mystery, preaching the kingdom, we touched upon a broader meaning of kingdom that comes to us from modern scholarship. The particular emphasis that I would bring, as a way to show how all the mysteries are interconnected, is to understand the kingdom as God's claim. While in the course of reflecting on the mysteries, we will return often to the metaphor of claim, so a few words of introduction are in order here.

Modern biblical discussion brings much light to bear on the metaphor of the kingdom. The language of kingdom, parables, and miracle stories, has been intensely studied. And with that study of the Gospels has come a lively awareness of the kingdom imagery in the Old Testament and in New Testament writings earlier than the Gospels. This body of research has led to a dynamic appreciation of the simple yet profound proclamation: the kingdom of God is in your midst!

Although used very frequently in the gospel presentations, the word *kingdom* is often a drawback for the modern reader because it is heard as territory. The word *reign* is more often used today because it connotes personal relationship. With this shift in emphasis, a window is opened to appreciate a greater shift that had already taken place. In the experience of exile and the loss of territory, postexilic Judaism looked not as much for territory as for a personal messiah. The description of the ideal king—for instance, in Psalm 72—is a reworking of symbols and images borrowed from the ancient Near East but nuanced to express Israel's covenanted relationship with God, which the king embodies. We see the same trend in the royal psalms when Yahweh is enthroned as king (Pss 93, 96, 97, 98). So looking to the past, we trace the

New Testament language of "kingdom as personal reign" back to the cherished expressions of Israel's faith and hope. Looking to the future, we recognize that the same symbol of the kingdom of God embraces the struggle for a more just world in solidarity with the poor, the agenda for the Christian church at the beginning of the twenty-first century.

To say that the kingdom of God is the guiding symbol of the Rosary is indeed saying a lot. Were this insight to be sustained upon reflection, it would make the Rosary an invaluable tool for a modern spirituality. Certainly were one to construct a template that bonds the symbol of the reign of God and the tenets of Catholic social teaching, those praying the Rosary would be blessed to find themselves in very good company. Their marching orders come from the famous six verbs, best translated in the present tense, of Mary's Magnificat (Luke 1:51–55) that announces very well the revolutionary agenda of the coming personal Messiah: "He *has shown* strength with his arm; he *has scattered* the proud in the thoughts of their hearts. He *has brought down* the powerful from their thrones, and *lifted up* the lowly; he *has filled* the hungry with good things, and *sent away* the rich empty."

What would be a link between the kingdom symbol and Catholic social teaching? I propose that the concept of "claim" links the symbol of the reign of God and Catholic social teaching. Why? To back up, the discussion has moved from kingdom (meaning territory) to kingship (meaning personal authority to reign). Thus, the verb *to reign* rather than the noun *kingdom* is stressed. I propose substituting the verb *to claim* for the verb *to reign*. "*Claim*" is particular and personalized. Most importantly, *claim* underscores the sense of personal relationship. This further shift is key to my presentation on the Rosary.

Moving from the word *reign* to *claim* helps us see the claim of God as an imposition of God's righteousness, that is, a celebration of God's personal covenant fidelity to us. God, as king and shepherd, is making good on promises to establish a new covenant. God has no other reason to be faithful other than because God is God. This is the feature of God's relationship with humankind and the world, whereby God acts to save us not for our sake but for God's own sake. God says, "I acted for the sake of my name" (Ezek 20:14; see also 20:9, 20:22, and 36:22). This convergence of images of God justifies a shift to the word *claim* to speak of God's action in regard to humankind and all creation. In Jesus, God makes the divine claim on all of creation that is even more dramatic when Jesus struggles with counter-claims. In the temptation scene, Satan makes a counter-claim on the interiority of Jesus. Jesus' repulse of the counter-claim of temptation—for that is what temptation is—is set in terms of the first commandment. "You shall worship the Lord your God, and him alone shall you serve" (Luke 4:8, from Deut 6:13).

To speak of the kingdom as the personal claim of God upon all of humankind and all of creation in all its diversity and richness, complication and fascination, brings us to the rich religious symbol of being made in the image of God. The celebration of the kingdom is an acknowledgment of God's claim upon God's own image. A mainstay in Catholic social teaching (but too often dryly interpreted), the idea that we are made in God's image evokes an appreciation for divine artistry and the passion with which God claims this image. What artist is indifferent to his or her image expressed in their art? Far from being indifferent, the God who is revealed in the Bible is committed, as passionately as a parent, to the works of God's hands. The prophets put us in touch with the pathos of God precisely by showing all humankind and creation as the endearing work of God's mind and heart.[19]

St. Paul is no stranger to this imagery and, in fact, advances the discussion greatly connecting image and glory (see 2 Cor 3:18—4:6; Phil 2:6, 3:10). The image of God mirrored in Christ is ever being formed in those who behold the glory of God on the face of Jesus. Thus image, form, glory, kingdom, reign, and claim can be seen to follow, one on the other, as we develop the cluster of symbols that can give us a template with which to contemplate the mysteries of Jesus. Each component has a definite emotionally charged setting in each of our human lives. One metaphor extends the other, and in the contemplation envisioned there is a constant surrender of yet another whole realm of human experience to the avalanche of God's love. The exploration of the human experiences that come to expression in each of these links makes our prayer of the Rosary an adventure in the rich and all-engaging world of the heart and the spirit.

This understanding of the mysteries of the Rosary can be aligned with what is called "emotional intelligence," a contemporary theory about being human. Emotional intelligence describes how a person comes to know a situation using all the powers of mind, spirit, psyche, and body.[20] If spirituality is an affective appropriation of our faith assertions, then an emotional intelligence is a prerequisite for that appropriation. It is commonplace to say that faith is "belief in"—that is, faith *in someone*—and is not to be confused with "a belief that." If it is reasonable to believe in a higher power, it is reasonable that that belief have a core that is personal, emotional, and intellectual, integrated with will, emotion, and mind. Although the exercise of religion may serve a political agenda and thus be, at times, distorted, one ought not deny its power to integrate. Genuine religion engages a person in the integration of his or her human life and helps a person come to a holistic grasp of him- or herself in relationship to a higher power. For Christians, God is personal and is revealed in the ministry, death, and resurrection of Jesus Christ. Jesus as Risen Lord is present to, with, and for us and calls for a total response of mind, heart, and spirit with him. Such never happens without involvement with others. This emotionally intelligent response is worked out in the plethora of images and symbols given to us through the faith assertions of the community.

The modern-day Christian is asked to believe, not on the strength of the religious experience of the early disciples two thousand years ago, but on the basis of his or her experience *today* that affirms and echoes the experience testified to in the texts of the movement. Christians today do not survive on a vicarious or pseudo-experience but on their own experience interpreted in the light of the tradition. This is testimony to the presence to each generation of the Risen Lord in the power of the Spirit. We can speak this way of the presence of the Risen Lord because of the pioneering work of the evangelists. John, especially, gives us an account in his Gospel that beautifully fuses together Jesus of Nazareth and Jesus as Risen Lord. He overlaid the foundation of the historical Jesus with the "already" of the Risen Lord so that he presents Jesus referring to himself as "I AM," the designation of God from the story of Moses in Exodus 14. But the narrative of John and of the other New Testament testimonies would never have been possible were it not for the continuing gift of the Spirit in the privileged setting of the community gathered to memorialize in praise and thanksgiving the death and resurrection of the Lord Jesus. As often as the Christian community gathers to do anything, but especially to celebrate Eucharist, it is always in the power of the Risen Lord that it gathers. Tragically, the religious experience of the Risen Lord is often downplayed and even made the object of suspicion. The battles over Christian doctrine and, indeed, over shared power between church and state, have contributed to the deprived way in which Christian doctrine is often presented. The intelligence that comes from one's emotions as key to the discernment of genuine religious experience has done much to correct this deprivation.[21]

Of course, for many, there never was an imbalance because they found in the praying of the Rosary not a battleground of dogma but an opportunity to cultivate holistically a relationship with Jesus. If there were an imbalance, it had to do with a disproportionate emphasis on the sufferings of Jesus and a failure to know Jesus, as St. Paul says, not only in the community of his sufferings but also in the power of the resurrection (see Phil 3:10). An understanding always existed that the sufferings of Jesus to which, out of his or her own personal experience, the person praying the Rosary related, was not the last word. However, God's last word in the raising of Jesus from the dead was often left outside the time and space of our human lives now. A well-balanced Christian faith would recognize both the end-time value of the final word of God and the anticipated, pilgrim value of God's final word for our journey now. Our life in the present is lived on the strength of that final word, given as the "down payment" on our inheritance in the resurrection (see Eph 1:14) and to be completed in the new heavens and earth of John's apocalyptic vision. Life is a valley of tears but not only a valley of tears. Emotions of grief and loss are often the stronger, but the Christian needs to nurture emotions around the "hope of glory" (see Rom

5:2 and Col 1:27). The person praying the Rosary develops the emotional connections between the template of our contemporary experience, in both its joys and struggles, and the template of the story revealed in the recitation of the Rosary. The Rosary is a series of interactions with the people who make up the story, and bonding with them becomes, over time, a trusted relationship. For instance, what do the words "ascending to my Father" of her friend Jesus mean to Mary of Magdala? Would I too have wept like Peter when the cock crowed a third time? How does my experience of the Risen Lord in the boat with the disciples relate to my fears of a disaster, a hurricane, a tsunami?[22]

Is building such an emotional connection with the disciples faithful to the text of scripture? The answer is "Yes!" When reading the Gospels, our eyes are fixed not only on Jesus but on the community telling the story. In telling the story and passing on the tradition, the community is painting a picture of itself in relationship to Jesus. Thus, for instance, in John 6:68, Peter's question "Lord, to whom can we go?" elicits a response from the mouth of Jesus that a wavering Johannine community was seeking in terms of remaining faithful. Reading the Bible is never a one-on-one exchange; it is more one process alongside another process of telling the story, of being a witness, of giving testimony. We share the faith convictions of those who gave us the text, and the text lives because of our common faith. To what questions were our brothers and sisters in the faith responding when they told the story that way? What are our questions today? Granted, we have few answers to the many questions that we bring to the text, but in asking those questions we open the text up and find in it a new context. This is what Paul VI called a co-naturality in faith between us today and those who gave us the text.[23]

We do not have to set our life aside to pray the Rosary. We learn to pick up the beads as we unabashedly are at any one moment. We are on a journey within a journey. We are pilgrims with pilgrims. The template of the one praying is shaped by ongoing human experience. Personally, my return to praying the Rosary came at a time when I was doing a lot of driving. So I relate well to the sense of a journey within a journey and to the various emotions not only of the journey but of the tasks underway.

These reflections promote a biblical spirituality based on a biblical theology. By that I mean a synthesis of insights flowing from an analytical reading of the text. Such analysis notices in a biblical passage elements such as biblical allusions and plot, and literary forms such as dialogue, parable, and miracle stories. Hopefully the task of synthesizing respects the identity of individual biblical writers and the structures of the biblical story in itself, not confusing one author with another nor imposing on the story ways of thinking that distort the Bible's own themes and concerns.

In mapping out the elements in a discussion of the Rosary, I have suggested how the practice of praying the Rosary may make us at home in the newer approaches to scriptures advocated by the teaching church. Also I have noted how the Rosary may inculcate a feeling for Catholic social teaching as intimately connected to the mysteries of our faith in response to the claim of the reign of God's love in Jesus. My approach to the mysteries of the Rosary will be likewise a flow of consciousness that might fit our contemplative spirits. The goal is to relate our faith to the ups and downs of our everyday lives. There will always be more that could have been said, and no one study can assess all the angles of what is called a compendium of the truths of our

Christian faith. However, one request I make in sharing these insights is this: Have your Bible close at hand when you read these reflections and check not only my references but add your own to them.

I return in the close of this introduction to a co-naturality in faith of which Paul VI spoke with great feeling. That is the play within the play, the journey within the journey, the conversation within the conversation, the contemplation within the contemplation, that bonds us in each other's story, and ultimately convinces us of "the breadth and length and height and depth, and to know the love of Christ that surpasses knowledge, so that you may be filled with all the fullness of God" (Eph 3:18–19). Take this text of Ephesians, with which John Paul II begins his reflection, as a commentary on the *Duc in altum*—put out into the deep (Luke 5:4)—the claim on us of the kingdom in the third millennium of our Christian faith.[24]

1

THE MYSTERIES
OF LIGHT

†

First Mystery of Light
THE BAPTISM OF JESUS IN THE JORDAN
Matthew 3:13–17, Luke 3:10–22

"...to fulfill all righteousness..."
(Matt 3:15)

In introducing the Mysteries of Light, or Luminous Mysteries, John Paul II noted that "the whole mystery of Christ is a mystery of light. He is 'the light of the world' (John 8:12). Yet this truth emerges, in a special way, during the years of his public life when he proclaims the Gospel of the kingdom."[1] In what ways is Jesus' baptism connected with the kingdom of God? If the kingdom of God can be understood as God's claim upon us in Jesus, then in what way is John's baptism of Jesus also a claim upon us? To enter the story with this question invites our contemplative participation.

Matthew's text handles a concern that is seen in the early traditions, to restate for the followers of John the Baptist the relationship between him and Jesus. There is also an apologetic understanding that ignorance of John is ignorance of Jesus, just as St. Jerome said that ignorance of scripture amounted to not knowing Jesus. As often as an evangelist responded to this early church dilemma of the identity of John, each evangelist added his own particular nuance. In Matthew's Gospel, John objects to baptizing Jesus, and Jesus responds: "Let it be so now; for it is proper for us in this way to fulfill all righteousness" (3:15).[2]

The word *righteousness* carried many meanings in the early Christian movement, as it also did within Matthew's Gospel. The word regularly refers to behavior, for instance, Joseph is a righteous man (1:19), in that he would not repudiate Mary, his betrothed; often it refers to relationship, just as when, in the judgment of Pilate's wife (27:19), Jesus is said to be a righteous man. These meanings are not opposed to each other. In describing John's baptism of Jesus as righteousness, Matthew may be eliciting a meaning closer to relationship than to behavior. Beyond the behavior of submitting to a baptism for repentance, Jesus is referring to his relationship with God in the plan of salvation. God is claiming his people in the ministry of Jesus, and this claim is immediately acknowledged in the voice from heaven: "This is my Son, the Beloved, with whom I am well pleased" (3:17). Jesus, who preaches that the kingdom of heaven is at hand (4:17), and who will go on to present that kingdom in the Sermon on the Mount (5:1—7:28), is himself the kingdom; that is to say, is himself the claim of God made upon us. His baptism by John is Jesus' submission to the claim of God laid upon his life. This is a constant theme in praying the Rosary, repeated often in the words of the Our Father: "Your kingdom come, your will be done"; in other words—Father, claim us as your own.

Efforts to correct misperceptions of the role John plays in the early movement served to underscore the actual vocation of John and, indeed, his perennial value. One could say that John was born to baptize Jesus, and in the light of this action, all the details of his life take on new meaning for the Christian. The role of John is highlighted as the pre-evangelizer when Jesus submits to the baptism of repentance. John's message of urgent repentance makes a claim upon Jesus. In responding, Jesus is actually fulfilling and, indeed, furthering God's promises. As the pattern of God's relationship in the Old Testament shows, every fulfillment is itself a further promise and inherent claim. In Jesus' fulfilling the promises of God, God is making further claims upon us. In Jesus' response to the preaching of John the Baptist, there is a fundamental claim laid upon our lives. John's preaching stresses our need for salvation, and so has lasting value. John the Baptist not only presents the need for salvation but also the faith that God will be faithful in turn by empowering us to respond. So, to sum up, God is righteous because God fulfills promises, and because God is faithful and fulfills promises, God makes a claim upon our allegiance. What profound mysteries of our faith are tied into the story of John! We celebrate the creativity and boldness with which God fulfills promises. For our part, the call to repentance (Matt 3:2) means totally turning around one's life to God in response, and being enabled to do so by the divine claim.

"What then should we do?"
(Luke 3:10–20, 21–22)

Luke brings to his presentation of John the Baptist the same gifts as a dramatist that he brings to other parts of the tradition handed on to him. Luke, like Matthew, appreciates that just as one cannot understand Jesus without a knowledge of the story of Israel, in the presentation of the Gospels, one cannot know Jesus without knowing John the Baptist. In his potent account of John, Luke not only gives John an extended family of typical Old Testament stock characters and a distinguished prophetic pedigree, but also he weaves in some of the concerns of the communities for which he was writing. While the urgency of the claim of God is well noted in the tradition that Matthew and Luke had in common (Matt 3:7–10, Luke 3:7–9), Luke applies that claim of God to a number of problems of his day.

In Luke 3:10, people ask John the Baptist "what then should we do?" If the Baptist is dramatized as fulfilling the expectations of God's covenant with Israel, it doesn't take much to find the concerns of this God of the poor and the exiled, the lost and the marginalized, represented in the demands of the Baptist. John's examples have to do with social justice, pointing out that God makes God's claim upon us in how we are to care for each other. He calls for solidarity with those who lack clothing and food and for the avoidance of the abuse of power by tax collectors and soldiers (Luke 3:10–14).

This call of John the Baptist for solidarity with people in need offers but another way to answer an ever-relevant question: if Jesus is without sin, why should Jesus submit to a baptism of repentance? Although it would be hard to find a commentary that does not address this question, each of us must come to our own satisfactory answer. And beneath that answer will be found many deeper understandings of how God saved us in the death and resurrection of Jesus. Or, put in the language of our reflection, how is the claim of God upon us and upon all creation worked out in the personal odyssey of Jesus of Nazareth? One aspect of the answer that this mystery of the Rosary suggests is again this key precept in Catholic social teaching: solidarity. Jesus of Nazareth may have been without sin, but he stood with us in our sinfulness and our need for forgiveness and salvation. In submitting to baptism by John, Jesus entered into the prayer for all humanity. On the cross Jesus prays for all when he says, "Father, forgive them; for they do not know what they are doing" (Luke 23:34). On the cross, Jesus is not only the solution; he submitted to the most painful effects of the originating problem. In his solidarity with us, Jesus held himself accountable for our sin.

Solidarity with others is a major template of our modern experience. Modern telecommunications enable us to know what is going on all over the world. This fact of being connected extends not only to those who are our contemporaries but also, I would emphasize, to those who preceded us in life. Many of the blessings we have today come from the efforts of those who preceded us; many of the difficulties—racism, for instance—come from the limited world view of those who preceded us. We may not be responsible for the sins of our ancestors, but we must be accountable. Too individualistic an understanding of responsibility would leave us saying, "Racism is not my problem: *I* do not discriminate." A Christian sense of solidarity would say, "We will obligate ourselves to take account of the racism that we have inherited from the past and that continues to afflict the family of humankind today."[3]

Significantly, Jesus used this sense of solidarity when in Matthew's Gospel (23:29–36) he indicts the Pharisees using their own words: "You say 'If we had lived in the days of our ancestors, we would not have taken part with them in shedding the blood of the prophets'" (v. 30). He takes to task the failure in the present to repudiate the shortcomings of the past. The argument that, had we lived in our ancestors' time, we would not have done such and such is belied by nonpractice now. The argument does not convince Jesus. A sense of solidarity with the effects of our ancestors' sins, Jesus claims, leads to a new accountability today. The same sense of solidarity gets extended in terms of the world's future that we prepare for those to come after us. Will we leave the world a better place, morally, ecologically, politically, than we found it?

It will come as no surprise that nurturing such a template of solidarity demands a lot of soul searching. Is it not already a struggle to own up to the implications of one's own hatred, envy, jealousy; racism, sexism, greed; discrimination against others, inaction against injustices, or cover-up in the face of sexual abuse? Why would we want to take on the sins of "our ancestors"? The answer is both/and: how our sin is the outcome of our present actions, and how our sin is the outcome of the past we would deny. Jesus' baptism in the Jordan forever unmasks our denial. In the divine testimony to Jesus—"You are my Son, the Beloved; with you I am well pleased" (Luke 3:22)—the baptism scene urges us to see in the death and resurrection of the Lord Jesus all the power and feeling of solidarity that is needed to undo the distortions of history and accept again the claim of God's graciousness in the present and for the future.

So we have the template of the righteousness of God, and the template of solidarity. What then do we bring to the Rosary? Is there anyone among us who has not been affected by the sins of our ancestors? And whose life does not likewise endanger another's future? Envision again John's contemplative symbol: "Here is the Lamb of God who takes away the sin of the world!" (John 1:29). John would have us hand over to the lamb, symbol of God's own covenant righteousness, our solidarity in the sin of the world.

†

Second Mystery of Light
THE MARRIAGE FEAST OF CANA
John 2:1–11

"Thus did he reveal his glory."
(John 2:11)

Only John, the fourth evangelist, gives us the story of the wedding feast of Cana. After the magnificent beginning in John's famous prologue, it is understandable that picking up the thread of the narrative is not easy. He places the story of Cana between that of the ministry of John the Baptist and the cleansing of the temple. These will be followed by Jesus' discourse with Nicodemus. John's Gospel seems tangled at this point like stories jockeying for position. As only becomes evident after several readings, from the beginning John assembles many characters, all of whom return at one point or another in the unfolding story. By the time the reader gets to John 21, he or she sees how each story added to the thematic richness of the gospel presentation. No gospel scroll was intended to be read just once; only in repeated readings and much contemplation does one come to grasp the deeper connections.

The invitation of modern biblical study, which I offer at this juncture, is to put on your three-dimensional glasses, and read the gospel text on three levels:

- the ministry of Jesus
- the early communities
- the level of the evangelist

The traditions, put down in writing, come from the disciples' memory of Jesus and his ministry. These are handed on by the early Christian communities, constantly being reshaped as they are handed on. Finally, the evangelists reworked those traditions for the good of the communities for whom they were writing but also, and primarily, to praise God by passing on the good news of our salvation. From a literary point of view, the level over which we have the best textual management is that of the evangelist. And because the communities for which the evangelist was writing accepted the work, we have to assume that they perceived the work as an adequate reflection of their contemplation. The Gospels, as the *fruit* of much contemplation, were *intended* for contemplation. And here contemplation has the full force of two templates being juxtaposed: what in the tradition needed to be handed on and what the community needed to hear in order to address its needs. To state the dynamic, this way is to leave the process very open, for there will always be new needs and horizons, and so there will always be a fresh rereading of the tradition.

The story of the marriage feast of Cana is surely the fruit of deep contemplation and it invites more. Within the gospel traditions, there are many parallels with this story and, within the plot of John, many ways that the story foreshadows later narrative events. Already in the traditions about John the Baptist, there were intimations of the arrival of the bridegroom, and the connection was made with putting new wine into new wineskins (see Mark 2:19). Within the Gospel of John, this simple story anticipates many elements further in the Gospel: a third day, the first sign in Cana, the presence of the mother of Jesus, the hour and the glory, and the all-important understanding, in John, of faith in the person of Jesus.

As we watch this young couple, joyful and eager to make a claim on each other's love, but anxious because their wedding feast may be remembered for lack of hospitality, we see an even greater claim being made by Jesus, not only in celebrating the gift of their love, but in responding to their anxiety. As if moving out in concentric circles from the presenting problem of having no wine, we encounter deeper and deeper meanings to the point that such a human exchange as marriage is fused with meanings that lead us to the brink of glory, the biggest claim of all on us as humans (John 2:11). John creates a trajectory of claims that spans out from marriage and its underlying significance: from the couple to the claim upon the family to offer hospitality, to the claim of faith in the wonderworker, to the claim of glory of the God who works through Jesus. The person of Jesus holds all these claims together, as stated in the words of his mother: "Do whatever he tells you." To obey Jesus is to give glory to God!

The story is often taken as Jesus blessing marriage. And why not? In a typical reversal of expectation that we will see later as key to the coming of the kingdom, the guest becomes the host. His presence lends dignity, care, and warmth to the scene, as well as a heightened significance of covenantal bonding with each other in God's plan of salvation. Thus the connection between Jesus and marriage was established to the point where later generations of Christians would say that Jesus instituted the sacrament of marriage, thereby giving to marriage, so natural and necessary, a transformative value.

A sacrament is in itself a contemplation, the coming together of two templates, two whole structures of life and significance. The action of the couple committing themselves to each other is the action of two lone persons who need to love and be loved, a template that brings together enormous dreams and expectations, unites families, touches the sacrosanct desire to continue the human family, and advances the prospect of an inheritance and the stewardship of the earth. The many meanings of this gifting of oneself to the other will be carried over into the action of God espousing the human family in the death and resurrection of Jesus, when Jesus' hour has come. This action of God is the anointing with glory, the energy that transforms the beholder; here, a frightened couple at the beginning of their life's journey together. Granted at the beginning of their life together, as at the beginning of John's story of Jesus, the revelation is more foreshadowing than total manifestation, more intuition than full knowledge.

Saying ten Hail Marys in one decade of the Rosary will never provide enough space to contemplate these realities. Marriage touches in so many ways what is fundamental to being human, and each of us will bring a ready list of people and situations to enrich the meditation. With each movement of the beads we realize the depth to which we can invite the claim of Jesus into the very detail of our human lives together. Everyone has a stake in good marriages, even the unmarried and those for whom marriage is, or was, an unpleasant experience. For some of us it is the recognition that, because we did not stay together, God did not put us together, and so, our template opens a chapter of sadness, perhaps of unreadiness for marriage or for liberation from an unhealthy relationship. We come to the contemplation of God's mysteries unfolding in our lives as we are, often broken, struggling, but never without "our hope of sharing the glory of God," to apply to John a Pauline phrase (Rom 5:2).

The story of the marriage of Cana lives. Many couples go to the town of Cana today to renew their marriage vows and buy a bottle of vintage wine. This is being true to the story because, despite the recognition of pain and struggle as was noted above, the thrust is toward the future and the desire that we do well in marriage. Many couples choose this passage in John for their marriage ceremony. The message often stated is this: The best is yet to come. Once again we are faced with a reversal of expectation: people don't expect the wine to get better as the feast goes along. Within the template of God, things that are already good just keep getting better. Knowing the goodness of the already-established covenant with God and using a typical Judaic phrase, we can say of faith in Christ, how much the more! We are glory-bound, and with such hope in our hearts, we contemplate the experience of glory in the present.[4]

✝

Third Mystery of Light

JESUS PREACHES THE KINGDOM
Matthew, Mark, Luke, and John

"For, in fact, the kingdom of God is among you."
(Luke 17:21)

In all four Gospels, Jesus preaches the kingdom. He is in himself the claim of God upon all creation and all humankind. The kingdom was not one other topic about which Jesus spoke. The kingdom of which he spoke and the power to which his presence pointed, was God's claim upon the hearer. If people followed Jesus, it was because they felt new power through him to live their human lives. And, so they had new hope. The word made flesh, the word made event of God that is central to the mission of Jesus, is an experience of empowerment. Thus, into the contemplation of this mystery of the Rosary—"Jesus preaches the kingdom"—we may bring a template known to us daily: the search for power. We bring a hunger to participate in life, to share power. I think that there's no greater hunger in our world today than the desire to share in the opportunities and advantages that modern life affords. Catholic social teaching sums up this desire in the word *participation* and already in Vatican II, we had the word *interdependence*.[5] Can a template of participation and interdependence find its counterpart in the preaching of Jesus?

All four canonical Gospels, John's Gospel no less than the Synoptics, present Jesus in and through the metaphor of the kingdom. From where does the metaphor come? Israel's history is greatly shaped by the stories of her kings, from the moment that Israel wanted a king (and God did not) to the point of hoping for a king who would be worthy of the God-given promises to the throne of David. To feel the passion over this search for a worthy king, one needs to pray the psalms—hence the Latin Church's emphasis on the Liturgy of the Hours. They draw together Israel's expectations of what the king should be and Judaism's compelling rehearing of those expectations after the experience of the exile.

The spirituality of Jesus of Nazareth is greatly influenced by the prayer rhythms of the psalms, the depth of emotion over Israel's inheritance, and the assurance that the lot of the "little guy" is important to God. One is therefore invited to interpret the ministry of Jesus proclaiming the kingdom in light of the psalms where the law, prophetic, and wisdom traditions of Israel intertwine.[6] Jesus' spirituality is shaped by the historical and cosmic dimensions that the psalms give to the cry for victory in the midst of the human struggle. The psalms are the script for Jesus and help him articulate the claim upon him to embrace his life's mission. Likewise, to understand Jesus, the early community turned most often to the Psalter. And when no appropriate wording could be found in the Psalter, Luke took the freedom to adapt wholesale in order to give us Mary's Magnificat. There, a key theme of the psalms, indeed of the whole life of Israel, which we already met in the story of Cana, is given stunning expression: the reversal of human expectation. Jesus came to turn the world upside down as is acknowledged by opponents of the Christian way in Thessalonica: "These people who have been turning the world upside down have come here also" (Acts 17:6).

King though he was, and with the intention to upend all things, Jesus came not in the splendor of royalty but in the plainness of little things, which made up everyday life. The derision of the Christian movement in the first centuries was in this sense deserved. Jesus announced the kingdom to all the wrong people: a long line of women subjected to prostitution, as well as tax collectors, insurrectionists, desperate widows, scruffy kids, and people too fearful to acclaim him in public. In time, of course, Jesus would speak to all: the high priest, the procurator, even Caesar, challenging his claims. But his heart was with the lowly, the outcast, the housebound, the distraught, and the demonized.

The Gospels are narrative portraits of this Jesus in terms of what he said, in terms of what he did, how he related to others, how he related to God. They are told retrospectively in the light of the resurrection.[7] The Christian reads the stories of Jesus' miracles and his many words therefore from two points of view: what Jesus said going forward, and what the church chooses to remember, looking backward. Every miracle story, therefore, is an anticipation of the resurrection, a preview of how God delivers on all the promises of Jesus. If Jesus is God's "yes" to all the promises to the ancestors (2 Cor 1:20), the revelation of the glory of God on the face of Jesus is God's "yes" to Jesus. Too often the words of Jesus about the kingdom, his parables in particular, are heard in a moralistic way. I do not think that this is their primary intent. I suggest that the parables and sayings of Jesus are to draw us into active contemplation of what life is like when we surrender to God's claim, when we find ourselves rejoicing with the neighbors because what was lost is now found, or when we see the wisdom in a shepherd's leaving ninety-nine to search for one stray lamb (Luke 15:1–10). Of course, even such outlandish imagination pales alongside the testimony of a Mary of Magdala: "I have seen the Lord" (John 20:18).

When the unimaginable got said in the parables, the intolerable got worked out in miracles.[8] The town clown is given access to the community of God's praise (Mark 5:1–20). The leprous Samaritan rewrites psalms of thanksgiving (Luke 17:11–19). The formulaic response to those whom the Baptist sent to Jesus to learn if he was the one to come, or if John should be on the lookout for another (Luke 17:22), explodes with new life on hearing the news of the resurrection (Acts 5:12–16). No, the resurrection is not best presented as the final proof that Jesus was divine, which was an argument in an earlier defense of the Christian faith. Rather, the resurrection is God's total approval of all the dreaming of a better and more just world that Jesus evoked in the heart of people. Miracle stories had the purpose of removing barriers, which are always mentioned in one way or another, and permitting people to participate, for participation was as much a dream for people then as it is for us today. The miracles and the parables were how Jesus invited us to dream with him. There would be no real claim of God upon all of creation, inclusive of humankind, if people were not able to participate.

Jesus often proclaimed the kingdom in the setting of table-companionship. He invited *all* to the table, even in a deserted place. He was often more open to strange guests than was his host. Many questioned his choices and refused his invitation. His sayings often address the hardness of those who fail to find in his invitation a key to resolving the suffering and exclusion of many. Jesus knew his adversary because many, as a way for themselves to survive, had used God to exclude others, using older religious traditions of clean and unclean. At times, even the majority were on the outside. Jesus protested such exclusion. In this kingdom outreach of Jesus, the early movement would see a way to open the good news to the Gentiles, to reinterpret understandings of clean and unclean, to invite all. (See Acts of the Apostles 10.)

Parable and miracle story, words and deeds, all make but one word-event! Isaiah already had spoken to this word-event when he said that no word of God ever returns to God without fulfilling the purpose for which God sent it (55:10–11). Such a word, always effective, makes an instant claim upon us, to which we respond eagerly or incur condemnation. People experienced Jesus' marvelous deeds as words that happen. His authority was different, and his word was command. He rebuked demons, and they obeyed him. He spoke with power, and persons were healed, even from afar. His presence created a crisis, a turning point. Believe him or be self-condemned. Surrender!

Just as we often interpret some event as an answer to prayer, one way to grapple with the experience of this man Jesus was to see him as the fulfillment of God's promise of a Messiah. The disciples whom he would meet on the road to Emmaus had come to hope that he was the one to redeem (Luke 24:21). The words of the prophets came alive in a new way. Indeed, a later generation of Christians would connect him with all the traditions of Israel and Judaism: in his wisdom, he did not come to abolish the Torah but to fulfill the prophets (see Matt 5:17). Trust him. If one cannot trust him, trust the God whom many were inclined to believe was at work in him. God's power was at work in him. Jesus came to *em*power, not *over*power.

Many more people heard the story of Jesus' healings than actually experienced the event. Many who were healed were themselves the narrators. The telling, often accompanied with further deeds, was a promise and fulfillment, a true experience of the word of God. Narration became a proclamation, making a claim. Proclamation of the Gospel, in making known the claim of God on us in Jesus, unmasks claims that do not liberate. So the Gospel is proclaimed in face of counter-claims. God's claim often clashes with the template of systems that promise what they cannot deliver. A huge chasm exists between the kingdom preached through empowerment in Jesus and the exploitation of the dispossessed in modern life by making promises with no commitment to follow through to fulfillment. Today modern telecommunications are our means of passing on stories and they often manipulate us, raising hopes but dashing promises. In selling to those who already "have," the very means of communication reminds those who "have not" of all that they lack. People now know what they are missing. It is not that people should not know but that the commitment to move rapidly to honestly sharing the goods of this world cannot lag behind. This is a commitment to an interdependent participative world about which Catholic social teaching speaks. The gap between word and event is the breeding ground of despair and violence. Christians, whose lives are shaped by the narratives of Jesus, word of God made flesh, will find in the proclamation of the kingdom the motivation and urgency to work with others for the development of all peoples.

In a whole new way, we hear the cry "How long?" of the ancient psalmist.[9] How long will the vast majority of the world's peoples live unempowered lives, in conditions known to be an insult to the dignity of the human being? How long can human potential be left underdeveloped? How long can the people of the world be divided into haves and have-nots? How long can religion, even the Christian religion, once the protagonist in the universal education of humankind, be content to educate the haves to the disadvantage of the have-nots? To the surprise of many Christians, the kingdom of God preached by Jesus is the coalescence of the claims of God on all God's creation and the claim of every human being to be respected and dignified! Jesus' equation of love of God with love of neighbor was already prefigured in the claim of the kingdom to treat all human beings with dignity.

One who prays this mystery of the Rosary will seldom move on to the next with any sense of completion. The call, the allure, the claim of God's power in the ministry of Jesus, proclaimed in the ministry of the church, are all-intrusive, pervasive, invasive, exhilarating, and inexhaustible. Jesus' parables are riddles to be resolved. Only by trusting Jesus' own juxtaposition of the template of his relatedness with God and the template of his relatedness with us in all our pain and struggle, can we hope to resolve the riddle. Ultimately the resurrection that illumines the death of Jesus is the parable-mystery of God's claim embryonically disclosed. Jesus' mission is to wrestle us back from Satan's host of false claims. Later we will see in the reflection on another mystery, Jesus' agony in the garden of temptations, how he struggles with claims counter to the claims of God upon his life. If, in such struggles, Jesus had said, as we often do today, "been there, done that," he would not have spoken proudly but truthfully. "If it is by the finger of God that I cast out the demons, then the kingdom of God has come to you" (Luke 11:20).

†

Fourth Mystery of Light

THE TRANSFIGURATION

*Matthew 17:1–8, Mark 9:2–8,
Luke 9:28–36*

"They saw his glory…"
(Luke 9:32)

The human face was a favorite image for John Paul II in his writings, perhaps because nothing is more expressive. Jesus' face (but not just his face) was transfigured before the disciples. All the Synoptics tell of the transfiguration of Jesus, and each sets the scene somewhere on the road to Jerusalem. The scene is sandwiched between two predictions of the passion and death.

Despite the transfiguration scene, Mark withholds the outcome of his Gospel—the revelation of the Messiah—until the end of the story through the confession of the Roman centurion at the foot of the cross: "Truly this man was God's Son!" (Mark 15:39).

By contrast, John does not have a transfiguration scene and does not need one. By layering in the outcome throughout the gospel plot, John presents Jesus as full of grace and glory from the beginning. If there is a transfiguration scene at all in John, it may be in the prayer of Jesus that concludes the discourse at the Last Supper (17:1–26). "The glory that you have given me I have given them" (22) is Jesus' prayer to the Father in respect to the disciples. Let glory do its work, and thus let the beholders be transformed (the ultimate prayer in any formation program). Make known to the disciples who I am, and let them be transfigured by the experience. To the end, Jesus remains the one who was sent that the world might believe, that we might have life, that the world might be loved, that the light might shine in the darkness, that the blind might have sight, that the dead might be raised, and that all might be born not again but out of the relationship that Jesus has with the Father from the beginning.

Jesus washed the disciples' feet that they might not only be cleansed, but transfigured. Nothing too ethereal about all this! And this service was presented as the command to love. John found a way to make an everyday occurrence—for example, foot-washing or a visit to the well—an experience transforming us into the glory that we already are. Glory is revelation. God was embracing the need of all human life to be revealed, to be known for who we really are. Our flesh is the revelation of God's word. John is unsurprisingly this-worldly and down to earth. The Alexandrians, a third-century school of Christian commentators, began a tradition of calling John's Gospel the "spiritual" gospel. If, by "spiritual," they meant unworldly, they were in error.[10] John's Gospel especially is worldly in that his presentation pushes us to see the deeper meaning behind the flesh. John's theme is revelation of God to humankind in the everyday language of our lives, the stuff of poetry and metaphor. Humankind is revealed to humankind, to himself and to herself. Jesus knew what was in the heart of people (3:24) and he told us everything we ever did (4:29)! He did not overcome the world to its vanishing but to its liberation (16:33), from the wine of Cana, to the bread of Capernaum, to the water of Gihon (John 7:37). Blood and water flowed from the pierced side of Jesus (John 19:31–37).

In the transfiguration of Jesus the disciples discover the effects of the kingdom. When God claims a human being, that person discovers who he or she really is. When God lays claim to the human family, we discover in Christ our dignity and purpose. Conversely, we can say, with St. Irenaeus of Lyons, that a human being is fully alive when he or she gives glory to God. We know from our own lives how a person, old or young, is transformed when he or she is noticed, cared for, loved. Is not the art of human communication built around the belief that every person is sacred and beautiful if we but put the time and effort into listening to them? If our love transforms another into the reality that he or she already is, how much more will God's love, foretasted in the love of neighbor, reveal our beauty and convince us that we are made for glory?

But why compare the theme of love in John's Gospel with the scenes of the transfiguration of Jesus in the Synoptics? How else to understand the introduction of Moses and Elijah into the story? The transfiguration of Jesus, the revelation to the disciples of who Jesus really is, God's testimony to him, takes place in the context of the long history of salvation, the history of the Law and the prophets, the gradual unfolding of the covenant relationship whereby God wooed Israel endlessly. In Luke, it is God's courtship (9:28–36) that Moses and Elijah were discussing with Jesus in terms of the "exodus" that was about to take place in Jerusalem. That long history comes to us in the claim of the kingdom that Jesus preaches, the claim that Jesus is the Chosen: "Listen to him" (Luke 9:35). Granted that the transfiguration is an anticipation of the glory of the Risen Lord—given, as many readers of the biblical text say, to encourage the disciples—it also connects paschal glory with the story of Jesus en route to Calvary. Some say, and not incorrectly, "no cross, no glory." But, to delve into a more radical meaning, indeed supported by John, the scene on the mount of transfiguration says the opposite: Without the hope of glory no one would ever undertake the cross. God is at work in Jesus, passionately pursuing the objective of making a new covenant with humankind and all creation. If the kingdom cannot be separated from the person of Jesus, God's covenant-making cannot be separated from the divine strategy of love. As Ezekiel 36:22 tells us, it is in loving us into new life and a new covenantal relationship that God manifests God's glory for no less a purpose than the revelation of God's name, for God's own sake! In this it is great to be God-forsaken!

Ironically, St. Peter wants to build three tents to avoid, say interpreters, having to resume the journey to Jerusalem and crucifixion. The one in whom the glory of God shines must suffer and be put to death. Jesus must be rejected. Were he not rejected, he would not have had to come. Jesus carries within him the "must" of the covenanted love of God. Such love embraces the rejection and transforms the resistance into obedience. Humankind was never the protagonist in this story of God's love for us. In this anticipation of the resurrection, the relationship that made possible this conspiracy of love for us is revealed: "This is my Son, the Beloved; listen to him!" (Mark 9:7 and parallels).

Each of the synoptic evangelists handed on the tradition with as few modifications as possible, recognizing that the tradition had already made the text exquisitely expressive of much that was core to their faith experience. When Jesus tells the disciples not to speak of the vision until the Son of Man is raised from the dead (Mark 9:9), the scene itself becomes a resurrection story. Now it is our resurrection story, our glimpse of glory on the road of trial and suffering, temptation and struggle. Life may have, ultimately, a happy outcome, but in the interim there is much that is tragic and painful. It is always fascinating to listen to people tell what held them together as they passed through the dark valley. In what did their glimpse of glory consist? Is it possible to hold on without sweet memory or some foretaste of glory? Were Moses and Elijah discussing the many ups and downs in the history of God's courtship with Israel, the pattern of death and resurrection the whole course of their careers? Were they talking over the times when God, fed up with his recalcitrant people, swore to destroy them but then repented of his anger and began again? Does God move from glory to glory on the basis of the intercessory prayer that argues that the divine majesty has more to lose than the petitioner in failing to answer? Isn't God only being true to Godself when God says that we will be saved for no other purpose than for the glory and praise of his name? Does God, in covenant making with us, put everything on the line? "This is my Son, the Beloved; listen to him!" Yes!

Reflection on the present, the actual "today" of our story, already suggests the template that we bring to the contemplation of this mystery. Luke insists on the relevance of the message each day of our lives in his repeated use of the simple but profound word "today." The more poignant aspect may not be the glimpse of glory ahead but the courage to resume the journey now. We need, as a good friend once told me, our minor resurrections on the road of life. Only the hope of another glimpse can get us back out there on any Monday morning. And it really doesn't help to offer glory at the end; we need glimpses of glory en route. Too many of the church's prayers promise heaven without adequately addressing the immediacy of this day, not only for bread but for glory, the revelation of beauty where we ourselves, as beholders, are transformed. The transfiguration was never intended to be a flight from the world. The spirituality of the Middle Ages may have legitimated a spirituality of flight in face of devastating plagues, plagues still visited upon the human family in many forms today. However, the trust of the transfiguration is the courage to endure in the present, taking one's place in the community of God's praise. That praise, the psalms would have us know, is always new and fresh after enduring the deep valley of lamentation and loss. Jesus' transfiguration anticipates glory but not to the silencing of the words of Psalm 22: "My God, my God, why have you forsaken me?"

Many who pray the Rosary are striving to hold it together for another "today." The invitation of this mystery is not only to rely on old glory but also to find strength in the new, fresh, vibrant praise of the psalmist who sings: "I cried out to you for help, / and you have healed me. / O LORD, you brought up my soul from Sheol, / restored me to life from among those gone down to the Pit. / Sing praises to the LORD, O you his faithful ones" (30:2–4). For many today, recovery from any type of addiction is a form of spirituality. The person in recovery knows the daily journey to the "Higher Power" and the need to share the journey. Many more as supporters are working the same 12 Steps alongside those struggling with problems of alcohol, drugs, and sexual addiction, all admitting our need for a tent of glory. The mystery of the Rosary to which we, grasped by the upward call of God in Christ (Phil 3:12–16), ever return, is the transfiguration. It is the message of Jesus' death and resurrection, concrete and sobering! In a word, he touched me.

†

Fifth Mystery of Light
JESUS INSTITUTES THE EUCHARIST
Matthew 26:26–29, Mark 14:22–25,
Luke 22:15–20, John 6

"...to whom can we go?"
(John 6:68)

As we move into this fifth Luminous Mystery of the Rosary, there is no more important focus than the person of Jesus who gives us the Eucharist. This focus is maintained, although in dry, technical language by the church, when we speak of the institution of the Eucharist by Jesus. This means that the Eucharist can never be understood apart from the person of Jesus. Everything we know, believe, and love about Jesus as Savior, Messiah, Lord, and Son of God finds resonance in the celebration of the Eucharist by which we wish our lives to be shaped. The template, which we bring to this mystery of the Rosary, is the same template we bring to our celebration. Our participation at Mass is the embrace of mystery, divine awesomeness at the core of our being. Each one who comes to Mass has made his or her peace with attempts to understand the meaning of the Eucharist, often having probed things that are similar in other religions and finding that only a personal commitment to Jesus Christ and his proclamation of the kingdom is relevant to the celebration.

If a great religion did not have its central belief accessible in some core experience, through its holy places, holy shrines, stories, exercises, and pilgrimages, its appeal would never be sustained. For the Christian, this core experience is a participative action, the eucharistic action of the entire community of faith, gathered in table-companionship to memorialize the death and resurrection of the Lord Jesus. This is a memory, which is also an experience now, of presence with us, presence to us, and a presence for us, as powerful, and as all-claiming upon us, as when God revealed God's name to Moses: "I AM WHO I AM" (Exod 3:14). John's Gospel celebrates the continuity between Jesus as Eucharist and Moses' experience.

> "Very truly I tell you, whoever believes in me has eternal life. I am the bread of life. Your ancestors ate the manna in the wilderness, and they died. This is the bread that comes down from heaven, so that one may eat of it and not die. I am the living bread that came down from heaven. Whoever eats of this bread will live forever; and the bread that I will give for the life of the world is my flesh." (John 6:47–51)

The experience was interactive then and it is interactive now. Jesus as Risen Lord still presses bread into our hands and invites us to eat; a cup of wine and bids us drink. The church's teachings, to explain how this can be, will always fall short. But then its value never depended on our ability to explain it but on our ability to leave our lives open to the experience of Jesus of Nazareth, Risen Lord. We share the confession of Thomas' "My Lord and my God!" (John 20:28) and the gripping recognition of identity through transformation in the cry of Mary of Magdala: "*Rabbouni*" (20:16).

In consort with the deepest probing of cross-cultural religious experience and philosophical analysis of religious language, the church has gleaned rich insight into the meaning of the Eucharist. Separated from the person of the Risen Lord and encounter with him, as God gives it to us to experience, the Eucharist is then falsely presented as magic, superstition, an object of scorn and derision, another example of things that look bizarre in the practice of religion. But grounded in a well-nurtured and ever-deepening relationship with him who is present to, for, and with us, the eucharistic celebration is always the sacramental symbol of the God who is "I AM" for us. The sacrament of God's real presence transfers into the most elemental categories of our human existence, our need to eat and drink, the powerful testimony of the human story in which Jesus recapitulates God's story with us and the universe. Following on the story of God with Israel and Judaism, Jesus pointed to a whole world of symbolic actions and gestures that relates to our everyday lives. Long before he ever sat at the table of the Last Supper, he had prepared in advance the minds and hearts of his followers for this way of being present with them. He preached the kingdom in the midst of our human lives. He ate and drank in people's homes and understood the struggle to put food on the table each day. He knew thirst and hunger. If the kingdom he preached was God's claim upon our lives in its most fundamental details, Jesus also knew how to choose the symbols that would deliver his power for life in this world and in his name. The bedrock of existence doesn't get any more basic than the need to eat and drink. How disconcertedly ordinary that we meet that need in egalitarian and respectful table-companionship, where, as a matter of strategy in his preaching God's claim upon us, the guest becomes the host!

For all its days, the church will struggle to understand, to defend, and to protect its foundational symbol. And rightly so, for Jesus, the founder, chose to funnel into the symbol of table-companionship the significance of his life, death, and resurrection. "Do this in remembrance of me" (Luke 22:19). Memory and claim have become one. The memory is of how he had been in our midst, washing feet and welcoming all. The claim is that his life and his final meal were anticipations in prophetic gesture, as sure to be passed on as God is alive, that the kingdom, God's claim, is already within us! Jesus' hosting of the final supper echoes God's hosting of Jesus. How did God host Jesus? By accepting Jesus' strategy of love in face of death-bearing resistance. Such divine acceptance is what we mean by sacrifice. Only God makes holy, only God sacrifices. In accepting Jesus' loving self-offering, God renders his offering holy, that is, as giving access to God's own presence. God makes Jesus priest as one through whom alone God gives access to God's presence. If memory and claim meet in the celebration of the Eucharist, it is on the weight of desire. Luke gives us this testimonial: "I have eagerly desired to eat this Passover with you before I suffer" (Luke 22:15). John reminds us of the food that Jesus has, namely, to do the will of the One who sent him, so that reaper and sower would rejoice together (John 4:34, 36).

So the story of Jesus instituting the Eucharist is the story of his life and spirituality as one who took on totally the condition of being human in celebration of God's relationship with him. As an interactive, participative response to the person of Jesus, the Eucharist is a surrender to the desire of Jesus to carry the saving will of his Father into the very fibers of our lives. The Eucharist as the action of the entire community—the risen, missionary body of Christ, doing what is its most characteristic action—is the source of everything else the community thinks and does. This mystery of the Rosary prepares us, over and over again, to bring the whole of who we are into this interactive exchange. There is no understanding apart from knowing Jesus. Therefore, answering the question "Who do you say that I am?" is a sure way to prepare for Sunday liturgy (Mark 8:27 and parallels; see also John 6:66–71, built around the question "To whom can we go?"). To the person who claims not to need community in order to know Jesus, the answer is found in the will of Jesus expressed in table-companionship in acceptance of the underlying reality that we are each other's body, both in the begetting and in the nurturing. Jesus imposes community not as an externally affixed duty, but because we need community to be conceived and to sustain our human life. The symbolic structure that Jesus, in dialogue with his religious background and his experience of human life, puts together for his movement is tied to our known needs and desires.

The story as we have it now comes to us from the early brothers and sisters in the Lord. Led by the Spirit, they remembered the details of Jesus' life in the light of faith, not to give us merely a record but the epic that is told for our salvation. Long before they recounted the story of the Last Supper, they were celebrating, in a variety of community settings, the "Lord's Supper" as they referred to their celebration of the Eucharist.[11] Like good and tasty cake, the development of the story of Jesus is multilayered. To cut through all the layers that blend into the story of the Last Supper, and to see how it carries so much meaning for the whole life of Jesus, is not only an enriching task but also a humbling one. The story is told in the context of the suffering, death, and resurrection of Jesus. And those levels reflect how the community is living at the time of the telling. Luke gives us a short farewell speech that relates to service within the community (Luke 22:21–38, especially 24–30). Mark shrouds the whole scene with a struggle to know who will betray Jesus (Mark 14:43, where Judas is identified; see 14:17–21), while Matthew (26:19) shows that nothing is left to caprice or chance but is the fulfillment of the word of a teacher who can be trusted. A contemplation evoked by the scenes of the Last Supper, reverberating themes of memory, claim, and desire, confronts the ambiguity of our daily companionship at table. While the psalmist bemoans the table companion who betrayed him (Ps 55:14, 41:10), the person praying the Rosary knows, too, the struggle to remain faithful to those with whom we share bread. Even the food we eat at Eucharist demands fidelity. If we traced the story behind the bread and the wine, from the day the seed was cast on the earth or the bramble was trimmed, to its final arrival at the church door, few scenarios asking for a review of social justice would be left out. And the hunger of millions challenges us as we eat, knowing now as we do that hunger in today's world has only one cause, our political mismanagement of our stewardship of the earth.

How can anyone carry all this reflection in his or her heart at the time of Eucharist? The Rosary is not the only way to prepare for Eucharist. But a regular journey over these mysteries will no doubt help to align the template of a hungry world with the template of the Eucharist. This prayerful alignment is a fruit of wisdom, the biblically promoted skill for living in this world and that, according to John, is celebrated in the Eucharist. In Jesus' sermon for his visit to the synagogue at Capernaum, John takes the language about wisdom in Israel's tradition—for example, Proverbs 9:1–6—and applies it to both Jesus as God's work and our response to his invitation (John 6:22–59). "I am the bread of life. Whoever comes to me will never be hungry, and whoever believes in me will never be thirsty" (6:35). If repetition is one way to learn, the habit of praying the Rosary is a skilled response to the perennial invitation of wisdom: taste and eat (Ps 34:8). Such, claims John, is the invitation of Jesus, prophet, sage, and king in his welcome to Eucharist.[12]

Jesus' sermon in John 6 was itself a response to people who wanted to make him king. As a king, he was under claim to care for the people in their hunger and abandonment. They recognized his anguish to feed them. God's love at work within Jesus always finds a way, shown in Jesus' exuberant response, "Make the people sit down," to the complaint of Philip: "Six months' wages would not buy enough bread for each of them to get a little" (John 6:7). John suggests that taking part in this table-companionship is the wisest way to feed a world. There is no fundamental human question left unanswered. John ends with Peter's question that radicalizes the meaning of the Eucharist: "…To whom can we go?

You have the words of eternal life" (68). Peter's question turns out to be a most common-sense response to the claims of Jesus upon the disciples: If communion with you is the wisest way to live in this world, who would want to go elsewhere?

2

THE SORROWFUL
MYSTERIES

†

First Sorrowful Mystery
JESUS AT GETHSEMANE
*Matthew 26:36–56,
Mark 14:32–52, Luke 22:39–46*

"Could you not keep awake one hour?"
(Mark 14:37)

In this reordering of the mysteries, the sorrowful ones follow immediately after the story of Jesus' giving of the Eucharist at the Last Supper, the anticipation in prophetic gesture of what would transpire on the next day. While John's Gospel does not have the agony in the garden, his closing line to the supper scene evokes the challenge ahead: "Rise, let us be on our way" (14:31). The alleluias, anticipating final glory, traditional at the end of a Passover supper, fade into what John ominously calls "night" (13:30). The temptations that beset the life of Jesus return in full force. While John carries the echo of the "I AM" controversies of earlier scenes and Matthew has Jesus in full control of events (Matt 26:52–56), Luke and Mark give us the feeling of struggle in the face of paralysis and betrayal. Mark, who does not give us the Our Father, tells the story of the garden and in a few sentences brings in elements of the prayer of Jesus, his yielding to God's will, his necessity to pray, and his being tested. Mark, who does not tell us the contents of the temptations at the beginning of the ministry of Jesus, would seem to suggest now that Jesus' greatest struggle was with the sleeping disciples. Mark is unrelenting in showing the uncomprehending state of the disciples, a playing-out, as it were, of their scene in the boat that ends with Jesus' question: "Do you not yet understand?" (Mark 8:21). Jesus is forsaken, left on his own. Lacking are the angels and wild beasts that were present when he was first tempted (1:13). In keeping with those who think that Mark wrote for a community in denial of the cross, I ask, Was Mark rebuking a church that left people to suffer and die on their own in the sporadic persecution of the Empire?

The garden of Gethsemane represents temptation, a struggle captured in the word "agony."[1] The reader of Luke would recall that at the end of the first temptation scene, the devil departed from him for a time (4:13). When Jesus was arrested (Luke 22:53), he remarked, "But this is your hour, and the power of darkness!" What is the struggle? Jesus is tempted. A temptation is a counter-claim. Who is making a claim on him other than God? In the first temptation scene, the devil showed Jesus, in a single instant, all the kingdoms of the earth, and then said, "To you I will give their glory and all this authority;…if you worship me" (Luke 4:5–7). What power? The devil explains "for it has been given over to me, and I give it to anyone I please" (4:6). In many places in scripture, for instance, in the Gospels and in the Book of

Revelations, that power is described. But the question remains: Whose power is it, and who did the handing over of this power to the devil?

Here we are faced with the deepest meaning of sin: to hand the power of our lives over to the devil. To be made in the image and likeness of God is to have power; to sin is to surrender that power to someone other than the One in whose image we are made. Jesus came to take back from the power of evil what we had given over by yielding to temptation. And he knew temptation firsthand. In preaching the kingdom of God, Jesus attacked the other kingdom put together by our acts of demonization. The devil symbolizes our distorted and abused power when we make demons of each other. Jesus came to "de-demonize" the world, to liberate the world, to empower human beings to move freely again. Every town had its Gerasenes demoniac (Mark 5:1–20). In story after story, we find Jesus not only driving out demons but also attacking the social forces that normalized the banishment of the afflicted. In questioning the Sabbath, Jesus found the structures of Law and temple inadequate to meet people's needs. The Law was meant to help people, but was misused to demonize them. In each miracle, Jesus is allowing people to take their place in the community of God's praise. The list of people who found themselves freed by Jesus from social stigma is long, and includes Mary of Magdala, Bartimaeus, Matthew, Zacchaeus, and others. So that many may claim this new ground in their lives, those who hand on the miracle stories relish filling in the details of geography, social standing, and marginalization.[2]

Jesus had handed the world an alternative vision of life as human, freed from the counter-claims. In his healings and words, many found a glimpse of a new way of being in this world. Such a liberation would not only trigger resistance from invested parties but bring Jesus face to face with the ugliness of counter-claim. He endured to the end the resistance to his own message of liberation and forgiveness. He would remain true to his faith in the God of Abraham, Isaac, and Jacob, the God witnessed to in the scriptures, that he cited freely in rejecting every temptation. His trust in God was great. Jesus did not leave it to the enemy to state the terms of the struggle. In the words of Paul, Jesus overcame evil with good, not evil with evil (Rom 12). Jesus would stand his ground on what Judaism's spirituality, rooted in the struggle of the innocent person, now unjustly accused. In the short run, he would lose out to the power structures, religious and political. In the long haul, Jesus will be known as never having compromised his mission.

Jesus' life is shown as a struggle the whole of his days. The struggle begins with the temptation following his baptism against taking up his mission, and returns as he hangs on the cross, now a temptation to quit his mission in his final hour. Taunts, derision, and mockery characterize the response of some present at the crucifixion. "Let him come down from the cross now and we will believe in him. He trusts in God: let God deliver him now, if he wants to; for he said, 'I am God's Son'" (Matt 27:42–43).

The counter-claim takes many forms. The Letter to the Hebrews says that Jesus was tested through what he suffered (2:18) and "although he was a Son, he learned obedience through what he suffered" (5:8).

The testing of Jesus in the garden of Gethsemane recalls, then, the deepest struggle of his life as a contest of wills. That struggle goes on, but now we see it in light of the outcome. In the resurrection, Jesus has gained a beachhead in the struggle against evil. Paul, as one born into Christ out of due time, was blessed with the ability to name the struggle in micro and macro terms, but always in the light of his experience of the Risen Lord. The whole of human history is set on a new course. The counter-claim increasingly loses its dominance over humankind and creation. Paul presents the Law as the pawn of evil, not because the Law was bad in itself, but because the Law in itself could not compete with our demons. What the observance of the Law of Moses *could not do* is now made possible through union in faith with Jesus. For Paul, death symbolizes the outcome of sin, the ineffectiveness of the Law, and the resurrection represented victory over sin and death.

The garden scene suggests a daring template. We *still* don't get it. What we are up against is enormous. We constantly underestimate the power of evil and the doggedness of the counter-claims upon us. In face of the persistent temptations, the Christian community is called to vigilant prayer with Jesus. In Mark's Gospel, the theme of vigilance is important. All the energy of an apocalyptic view of the world, as presented in Mark 13, is channeled into the challenge of Christian vigilance: "What I say to you, I say to all: Keep awake" (13:37). Note how in the garden scene in Mark, the urgent plea "Keep awake and pray that you may not come into the time of trial" (14:38) echoes the petition of the Our Father in Matthew: "Do not bring us to the time of trial, but rescue us from the evil one" (6:13).

For his part, Luke claims that the struggle cannot be undertaken using the normal weapons of war. Thus Luke is particularly focused on refusing the use of the sword. Jesus sighs. He is resigned to the fact that the disciples will take a long time to figure out the futility of engaging in the right battle with the wrong armaments. I take the words "It is enough" (22:38) to mean "You just don't get it" when the disciples "take literally what was intended as figurative language about being prepared to face the world's hostility."[3] We will see later in the Joyful Mysteries, in Simeon's statement to Mary, the internal turmoil symbolized by the sword.

The contemplation called for in this mystery of the Rosary is on endurance when meeting temptation. Jesus was recalled as the one who endured the cross, for the sake of the joy that lay before him (Heb 12:2–3). The author of Hebrews goes on to ask that the readers "consider him who endured such hostility against himself from sinners, so that you may not grow weary or lose heart" (12:3). In the early communities, endurance emerged as a much-needed grace over against the continuing experience of sin. Yes, to the dismay of many, sinfulness has remained a part of Christians' lives in the world and even at times within the church. Endurance therefore is called for to spite the sin of the world and to confront the menacing ways in which sin entered the community from worldliness, causing backsliding, and a struggle for position and power. Christians knew, from the earliest literature—Paul's First Letter to the Thessalonians—that the struggle meant they lived in the final times. As the waiting persisted and more and more Christians died, no longer was the concern that the Lord's return was delayed, but rather the conviction that, in Jesus Christ, God has spoken for all time for us and the struggle was engaged forever. In Jesus' ministry, his presence provoked the demonized to shriek and cry out in protest when he drove out demons and thus laid siege to the reign of sin (Mark 1:24).

That struggle continues. If we do not experience our Christian life as struggle with temptation, it may be that we still do not get it. Are we failing to "keep awake" (Mark 13:37)? Are we becoming immune to the disvalues, disrespect, and indignities that surround us? We are called through our baptism to develop a value-centered consciousness in order to detect and combat the subtle ways in which we have surrendered the world to the power of evil. The Christian community, in its quest for social justice and the liberation of the oppressed and cursed by society, cannot expect less than the jealousy and envy of the evil one. Only by the lively and relevant celebration of Eucharist in the community can we be empowered to hold the line against this envy and jealousy with an enduring love, even to the point of shedding blood (Heb 12:4).

†

Second Sorrowful Mystery
JESUS IS SCOURGED
Matthew 27:26, Mark 15:15, Luke 23:16

"I will therefore have him flogged and release him."
(Luke 23:16)

The most negatively critiqued part of Mel Gibson's controversial film *The Passion of the Christ* was the scene of Jesus being scourged. For some, the ambiguity of physical violence reasserts itself. Ultimately, the ineffectiveness of all physically violent responses to human dilemmas is revealed. But was it Gibson's intention to glorify violence or vilify it? Did Gibson intend to reveal its ultimate futility? Was he trying to legitimate the well-documented return to torture as an acceptable way of obtaining information from captives? Gibson was far removed from the modesty of the New Testament on the sufferings of Jesus that are handled in the past tense. Gibson, it seems, is confused as to where the saving character of suffering lies. For me, and I think for many others, the only way to endure the long scene of the scourging of Jesus was to contemplate the many known examples of torture in our world today.

Matthew (27:26) and Mark (15:15) tell us that Jesus was flogged before he was crucified. However, Luke averted his eyes, as did many viewers during Gibson's movie. Luke intimates that Pilate would have Jesus flogged before releasing him (23:16). But the focus for the New Testament is not on the physical torture but on the endurance of the victim. To appreciate the emphasis on endurance, one will have to read Psalm 22 and Psalm 69, psalms that helped the early Christians to understand the sufferings of Jesus. These discreet references to suffering help supply what the evangelists omit. The message is that, under suffering, Jesus more than ever yields to God's claim upon him. Thus the depth of his spirituality, rooted in profound trust that God would not abandon him, comes through in the silent contemplation of his desecrated body. The breadth and length, height and depth (Eph 3:18) of his saving power is not measured in the excesses of the physical violence he suffered but in the depth of his love whereby he surrendered all to his relationship with God.

The tragedy of the passion narrative is that good people legitimated the violence. Were it a struggle between bad and good people, individuals caught up in their own sins, the tragedy would indeed be great. But, taking people to be sincere, the focus falls on religious systems. Only upon later reflection does the insight emerge that a blind reliance on the system put the Lord of Life to death. Paul seems to know an early reflection along these lines when he casts the matter in terms of wisdom. He speaks of the rulers of this age in a contrary-to-fact condition: if the rulers of this age had known. "But we speak of God's wisdom, secret and hidden, which God decreed before the ages for our glory. None of the rulers of this age understood this; for if they had, they would not have crucified the Lord of glory" (1 Cor 2:7–8). While this argument that people acted out of ignorance was already known in the early community (Acts 3:17), a later tradition, captured in John 16:2, deepens the motivation: "An hour is coming when those who kill you will think that by doing so they are offering worship to God."

This Rosary mystery of the sufferings of Jesus acts as a crossover to many insights into our contemporary experience, particularly an ingrained reliance on systems without a corresponding willingness to question all authority when it resorts to physical violence to attain its goals. The way we are entertained—violence in the movies, in video games, and even in the lyrics of our songs—conditions us to turn a blind eye to the use of torture. Nonetheless, many people of the United States today are shocked that our government rewrites international rules to legitimate our resort to torture and abuse, even sexual abuse of prisoners. Were one to number all the industries around the world involved in the production of instruments of torture, most persons would be shocked and saddened. Many, for the sake of a livelihood, blithely involve themselves in this production. The Christian community must take accountability, too, for the times that it has used physical violence against persons deemed heretical. When in the Jubilee Year 2000 John Paul II confessed these excesses and asked forgiveness for these travesties, some were slow to see his point and understand the depth of the violation of human dignity that they represented. It may well be because of torture in the name of God that a new interreligious dialogue can begin. Can there be hope that the voice of ordinary people will be heard, the voices of the mothers of "the disappeared," a re-echo of the Holocaust in the made-for-television genocides, the cries of those condemned to torture? With modern communication and a new willingness to question any abuse of authority, the excuse "we did not know" grows thin.

In John's passion narrative (18:28—19:16), there is a serious rebuttal of this abuse of power. Pilate's political calculations are indexed over against his misuse of power and his arrogant assumption of having no one to whom he is answerable. Pilate's intention bespeaks a politically motivated callousness to the situation of the sufferer. For scourging and torture can only be legitimated on a false assumption of a power that nobody has. Authority is the interpretation of power, and when power is misused to abuse others, this can only be a perversion of authority. Was there ever a time in the history of humankind where the use of physical violence for political gain was not in the forefront of political solutions? This violence and its legitimation in warfare was not only part of Israel's history but the subject of many debates within both Israel and Judaism. First there was an attempt to limit violence by placing all war booty out of human control. Then there was a movement to eliminate all violence. The prophets raised innumerable objections to violence, ridiculed Israel's attempt to mimic other nations by depending on the instruments of war, and moved the discussion, more and more, into the realm of divine action to remove violence from the realm of human action (see Isa 31). To claim God's causality of violence moves to its eventual elimination (see Deut 32:35, Rom 12:19).

Whatever was good and needed to be defended and protected would be taken care of by a provident and nonviolent God. Not only was the concept of the "holy war" a way to limit the violence, but the passion history of the individual prophets encouraged persons to endure violence rather than inflict it.[4] Ultimately, the prophet Jesus would show the bankruptcy of all physical violence that precipitated his own death. The scourging of Jesus comes at the end of a very long process of purification and self-knowledge on Israel's part. Therefore, it is to be interpreted as a further step in the long history of unmasking physical violence for the corrupt response that it is to human difficulties. When Jesus was vindicated in his being raised to glory, his scourging and torture were exposed for their distortedness. His treatment was the source of immense tension within the Jewish-Christian community. His vindication is a sign of hope to those who are victimized by the blindness and cruelty of others. There's no more water to wash Pilate's hands.

Today the story of his scourging urges us who pray the Rosary to examine the whole of our lives to know where we are complacent and fail to raise our voices in lamentation and protest over any and all violent ways of dealing with God's people. As the Father stands up for his Son Jesus, we too, in the power of the Risen Lord, take a totally unambiguous stand against all violence. There is never a day when that claim upon us is not very near and very urgent. This is where praying the Rosary and inculcating a social-justice spirituality come together. In order to be Christian, the contemplation of physical violence and the scourging of Jesus must move us to act. Such action is often ridiculed as naïve, but, in fact, there is nothing more naïve than to think that human beings can solve their problems by violence.

The sense of being violated is handed on through blood and ballads, and the violation of a people has profound ramifications for generations to come. Many of today's world hatreds stem from violations committed many decades ago. Economic violations and exploitations of another's resources can be successfully brought to some state of reconciliation, but the violation of persons burns for a very long time. The reconciling action demands immense patience and capacity to enter the pain of the one violated. Only the violated can do the reconciling, although many can help to bring that bold and daring action to pass. There have been remarkable stories of persons forgiving those who have "scourged" them. Each discovery of the futility of meeting violence with violence is itself a story of deep interiority. That interiority does not come about by denying the need for revenge but by transforming that need into energy that is life-giving and liberating for both victim and perpetrator.[5]

The perpetrator is victimized as well and needs a long process of healing and reconciliation. The scars of those who have scourged people from a distance made possible by modern arms, above the clouds and out of sight, haunt many veteran soldiers and contribute deeply to the breakdown in mental health and the rise of drug abuse. Likewise, by reflecting on the violence done to a living being through abortion, a fact seldom adverted to before the operation, many men and women recognized the other side of ending a pregnancy. The legal acceptance subverts the realization that a physically violent act is allowed in an environment that was meant to be the safest of all, the womb of a child's mother. There is a long healing process called for when this later consciousness of physical violence overcomes any subjective conditioning of the parents who availed of the procedure.

For one who has meditated deeply on the sufferings of the human condition, the sparse telling of the scourging of Jesus is sufficient to touch into that emotive intelligence that eschews all violence and all sanction of violence under any pretext. "Violence is a lie," the pope said in Drogheda, Ireland, in 1979 and repeated at the beginning of 2005.[6] It is no surprise then how rapidly John Paul II moves from this Rosary mystery of the abuse of power to the closely aligned mystery of a mock enthronement with a crown of thorns.

†

Third Sorrowful Mystery

JESUS IS CROWNED WITH THORNS

Matthew 27:28–31, Mark 15:17–20, John 19:1–5

"Here is the man…"
(John 19:5)

Luke skips details or rearranges materials to protect the disciples from too critical a judgment against them, and, more importantly, because he cannot bear to see his master hurt. So, in Luke, the detail of the crowning with thorns is passed over. Moreover, Luke presents Jesus as innocent, declared such repeatedly by many different persons. In telling the story of Jesus, Luke's eyes are fixed on the situation of the communities for whom he is writing. Matthew and Mark both refer to the crowning with thorns as part of the mocking of Jesus by the soldiers.

70

The scene occurs between Pilate's handing over of Jesus to be crucified and the commencement of walking the road to Golgotha.

The merging of two motifs, humiliation and enthronement, reminds one of how kings, as representatives of their people, were understood in the royal ideology in the ancient Near East. The king was considered the corporate personality of the society, and he carried the good and the bad for the whole of society. This was ritualized in temple ceremonies. In humiliating the king, a feature in the religious ritual of welcoming a new year, the people purged themselves of the bad things that had come to them in the previous year. Perhaps it is too much of an imaginative stretch to see in the mocking of Jesus the remnants of some ancient rite. The gospel reader, however, will not be surprised that the crowning with thorns of Jesus—who is God's claim, as God's messiah—will be presented in highly stylized ways.

The mocking is described in detail in Matthew 27:27–31 in two parts with five segments in each: stripping of clothing, putting on a scarlet robe, plaiting a crown of thorns, putting it on the victim's head, and placing a reed in his right hand (27:28–31). After the soldiers knelt and jeered at him saying "Hail, King of the Jews," they spat on him, took the reed, struck him on the head, stripped him of the robe, and redressed him in his own garments. The attention to detail clearly gives evidence of the deliberateness with which Jesus is presented as badly treated by Pilate's soldiers. In telling of the ridicule of Jesus, the New Testament authors create great irony. What the soldiers are doing, out of boredom and for the sake of entertainment, carries a much deeper meaning for the Christian reader. In the soldiers' derision of Jesus' claim to be a king, the Christian sees how Jesus *is* a king, in a reversal of normal expectations of royal dignity.

Although the crowning with thorns was undoubtedly excruciating, the emphasis of the New Testament is on the significance of the crowning. In Matthew and Mark, this is through the ironic humiliation of Jesus; in John this significance is carried much further into an enthronement of Jesus on the cross. He is the King. This significance is confirmed a scene later when the inscription of the cross, "Jesus of Nazareth, the King of the Jews," is allowed to stay by none other than Pilate (19:19–22).

John's elaboration of the scene before Pilate (18:28—19:16) is as carefully worked out as Matthew's. John re-echoes a number of the dialogues on the claims of Jesus. In response to Pilate's question "Where are you from?" (19:9), the exchange between Pilate and Jesus escalates into questions of origin and power. Pilate, although threatened by the presence of Jesus, cleverly declares Jesus innocent. Because of Jesus' own claim to be the Son of God, the leaders want to crucify him. Without access to capital punishment, they have no way to fulfill their own law. In order to fulfill the law that says that a blasphemer must die, the Jewish leaders hand Jesus over to the Roman procurator to have Jesus put to death. They are therefore at the mercy of Pilate, who exploits the situation so adroitly that he gets the chief priests to declare that "we have no king but the emperor" (19:15). Pilate can only be imagined as gloating upon hearing this huge concession from their mouths. The choice is stark: either accept the claim that Jesus makes upon you or end up declaring something that would be alien to the faithful son or daughter of Abraham.

What does the postmodern person praying the Rosary bring to the contemplation of this mystery? Faith. Faith is a crisis. Faith to accept who Jesus is, and from where he comes, is surely a gift but is also always a turning point. In place of living the Law of

Judaism within the context of Caesar's political power, the new
condition for the Christian is living political power within the
context of faith in the One who is from above. To live "from
above"—that is, to live human life out of the relationship that
Jesus has with God, as was enunciated in the conversation with
Nicodemus (John 3:1–21, especially 3)—is the context within
which to exercise political power. For the Christian, life in the
political realm is lived out of the claim that God makes upon us
in Jesus. However, such faith carries a political dimension if one
is beholden to the state for the living of the faith. But how can one
survive in this world without reliance on the state? No one is an
island, John Donne tells us, yet the claim of civil government cannot be ultimate. The question is where does power come from?
Even Caesar's power is derived. He would have none were it not
"from above" (19:11).

Pilate asks Jesus if he is a king (18:33, 37). The response to
this question brings two thematic images of the Gospel together,
king and shepherd. Earlier in the story, Jesus fled rather than be
declared king (John 6:15). Now he is willing to accept the title.
Jesus is the good shepherd whose voice is heard: "Everyone who
belongs to the truth listens to my voice" (see also 10:3, 16). This
response establishes how he is a shepherd king. Now he qualita-
tively discloses his kingship to the emperor's representative. He
is a shepherd king who lays down his life for the sheep (10:11).
The issue for Jesus is not to claim a title for himself but to claim
for his followers—indeed, all humankind—empowerment.

While all the Gospels tell the story of Jesus' kingdom-claim,
John's passion narrative develops the claim in terms of the most
radical sense of being human. Pilate says, "Here is the man"
(John 19:5), a neutral statement perhaps for the Roman leader

but one of increasing importance for the developing Christian community. It is in this man, guiltless, mocked, humiliated, that we find the true meaning of being human and what ought to be the significance of a crown on anyone's head: the willingness to give all, that there may be life and life more abundantly (John 10:10). Jesus stands alongside every human failed by systems intended to assist but incapable of abundant life. The scene before Pilate is searing theater at its best, an effigy of abusive power. The crown that Jesus wears is costly, but there is no greater love (15:13).

Pilate's words "Here is the man" (19:5) are, for me, a commentary on Psalm 8 or, more precisely, a commentary on the psalmist's response to his own question. The question is, "What are human beings that you are mindful of them, / mortals that you care for them?" The psalmist's answer is, "Yet you have made them a little lower than God, / and crowned them with glory and honor" (vv. 4–5). Jesus, shown to the people in "Here is the man," crowned with glory and honor, is the definitive answer to the psalmist's question. As the shepherd king, he suffered, died, and was raised for only one purpose: in laying down his life for the sheep, he loves every human being, even his enemy. Nothing shows the dignity of the human person more clearly than dying for love of an enemy, the very ones who are putting him or her to death. Persons who dispute the legitimacy of a social reading of the Gospel have to ponder this scene of crowning in John's Gospel. If the reign of any human king has any meaning, it must be in service of the dignity of human beings established in the crowning of Jesus, the shepherd king. "You would have no power over me unless it had been given you from above" (19:11). How it is given from above? Hear his voice.

Lest this reflection on human dignity be understood as an overemphasis on the place of humanity to the detriment of the rest of creation, one has to recall John's use of "all," a not insignificant word that occurs very often from the prologue to the prayer of chapter 17. (See, among other places, 1:3, 6:39–40, and 17:2, 7, and 10; in v. 7, the word *all* is sometimes translated "everything".) In recalling the words of Genesis, "In the beginning...," John honors creation. He brings this confession to a new level in "the word became flesh" (1:14), which anticipates the statement of Pilate: "Here is the man." In the journey from "the word became flesh" to "Here is the man," the reader learns from John how a human being should use power in the ecology of all creation. Catholic social teaching today finds in John an ally of extraordinary insight who, with one line in a biblical scene—"Here is the man"—presents a new place for humankind in "all."

Crowns are not a thing of the past. The verb *to crown* is used often in everyday speech even to the point of commercializing beauty pageants. This form of ranking is not without its value in the interpretation of Psalm 8 as we have chosen to reread it in light of Pilate's command to behold Jesus, " *Ecce homo.*" In fact, in Jesus we celebrate a coronation of humankind not in terms of heredities and entitlement but in virtue of the love with which he lays down his life for the sheep. Not only is the crucifixion scene in John's Gospel a coronation but also a beauty pageant apparent to those who look upon the one lifted up with faith (John 3:14–15, Num 21:4–9, and Wis 16:5–7).

Of course, the person praying the Rosary will not deny that the road to becoming a fully alive human being has its share of tears and thorns. Suffering is neither eschewed nor chosen for itself. How can we move from where we are to where we want to be, crowned as "a little lower than God," without suffering the resistance and the struggle that Jesus himself knew? The endurance, in face of this resistance, is well symbolized in the thorns that mark the particular crown with which Jesus is acknowledged as king. If suffering can have any meaning, it is because it is endured for the sake of an overwhelming purpose. John unequivocally shows that the purpose of Jesus' life is doing the will of the One who sent him (4:34).

Luke omits the crowning with thorns, but he does insist, in words his Hellenistic audience would understand, on endurance for the sake of an overwhelming purpose. Jesus lives in response to the necessity of God. The reader of Luke encounters the word "must" many times, already in the story of Jesus staying behind in the temple (2:49), to one final time in the Emmaus story (24:7) . We are faced with a battle of wills, and in place of saying that Pilate handed Jesus over to be crucified, Luke notes that Pilate handed Jesus over "as they wished" (23:25). The crowning with thorns, although seemingly an image of passivity, is in fact one of great will to endure. Everyone tries to enter the kingdom of God by force (Luke 16:16, Matt 11:12). This enigmatic saying takes its meaning from the life of Jesus. Only the will to endure, rooted in a faithful discipleship with Jesus, robs the counter-claims to the kingdom of their force and influence. The theme of endurance, "my word of patient endurance" (Rev 3:10), which I translate as "a strategy of endurance," is celebrated in huge and elaborate ways in the Book of Revelation, prominently when John introduces himself as "I, John, your brother who share with you in Jesus the persecution and the kingdom and the patient endurance" (1:9).

The story of Jesus lifts those who, although for a time may have to suffer violence, finally, by their endurance and hope of vindication, bankrupt violence and rob it of its power. The modesty of the New Testament is instructive. While not refusing to name the disease of violence and show its tentacles in every part of life, a restraint and a nonsensationalizing tactic is used in portraying it. The story, especially the words "Here is the man," is an invitation to the community to address the issues of violence, particularly domestic violence. In perpetrating violence, physical and psychological, violent people try to rob another person of their feelings of being human. *Ecce homo.* "Behold the man." This can often be read as "behold the woman," "behold the child," as one calls on the compassion of the community to mobilize forces to address the needs of the victims of violence.

This mystery of the Rosary inspires such a response. That inspiration is sufficient to begin a chain of reactions to help a victimized person in a proactive way. The Rosary is made up of a chain of short prayers, fueled by an encompassing vision of the claim of the kingdom. So, too, the resistance to a world built on violence comes from a whole series of clearly intended, small actions that effectively change mindsets.

No one will claim that praying the Rosary is a substitute for practical involvement. It shares with practices in many religions simply the art of slowing down, taking stock, and allowing oneself to become absorbed in the mystery of another. The commitment to the protection of children, on the other hand, as a response to their sexual abuse by clergy, is long term. No single fast, no single weekend retreat, will undo the damage done in the long grooming process that made the violations possible.

When in 2002, John Paul II spoke of the terrible iniquity of the sexual abuse of children, he used an expression from 2 Thessalonians 2:7: *"mysterium iniquitatis,"* the "mystery of lawlessness" He was laying siege to a very unsightly aspect of human life, but he was misunderstood. In using the word *mystery* the pope was not denying what is criminal activity nor promoting ignorance of mandated reporting. He was speaking of something beyond our understanding, too great for words, about the capacity of humans to do unspeakably cruel things against each other. Untold abuse, torture, and suffering have been legitimated by institutions, family, church, and state. To bring, over the course of time, our experiences of this dark side of human life to our Rosary invites us to draw, from the endurance of Jesus in his coronation and enthronement, empathy with the victim, and passion to safeguard against the manipulation within power relationships that results in violent abuse of others.

†

Fourth Sorrowful Mystery
JESUS CARRIES THE CROSS
*Matthew 27:31–32, Mark 15:20–21,
Luke 23:26–32*

"…fall on us…"
(Luke 23:30)

In praying this mystery of the Rosary, two important practices known to Catholic Christian identity, the Rosary and the Stations of the Cross, come together. One thing they share in common is the rhetorical character of religious imagery, an aspect that engages our attention many times. Through compelling narrative, the evangelist engages the feelings of the hearer and persuades the reader to get involved. Rhetoric, according to Aristotle, is the art of persuasion. The scene of Jesus carrying the cross is persuasive since it seldom fails to elicit participation. The time of being a bystander is over, the role of spectator is done. It is time to put away passivity and move into a community on the path to the cross. It is time to be a contemplative in action.[7]

Mark wrote to highlight the reality of resistance to the message of the Gospel. This means the centrality of the cross and thus the necessity to combat the tendency of some early Christians to emphasize glory to the eclipse of the cross. Had a Pauline insistence on the cosmic Christ, the firstborn of the new creation, eroded a sense of the centrality of the cross in the message of the Christian movement? Mark responds by giving us again the brute facts. In his unsparing starkness, he holds off to the moment of the crucifixion any human acknowledgment of who Jesus is. The Roman soldier says, "Truly this man was God's Son!" (15:39). Only then is disclosed the secret of who Jesus truly is. The light of the resurrection was not intended to erase the memory of the cross but to see, from the side of hope, its shape in every detail of our lives. Such has been the great contribution of Luke.

Luke has developed the journey motif that he took from common tradition and, indeed, from the journey tradition of the Old Testament, be it from Egypt to Israel or from exile home. Luke has marshaled his traditions into one journey to Jerusalem, a journey already foreshadowed in Jesus' visit to Jerusalem as a child. Indeed, the journey goes beyond Jerusalem to Rome. The journey with the cross is therefore a journey within a journey within a journey! The disciple, too, is on a journey and is told to take up his or her cross *daily* and follow Jesus (Luke 9:23).

When I worked in the inner city of New Bedford, Massachusetts, a number of churches organized a public Lenten Stations of the Cross. We chose to stop and pray at places that put us in touch with the pain of the world. In one neighborhood we lamented the lack of proper housing, in another the struggle to educate in the inner city, in another the struggle to live decently where drug dealing and use are rampant. We included on our route a center for the ecumenical movement and the grounds of the local synagogue to grieve the Holocaust. Many who saw us move from place to place seemed to understand a journey within a journey, a paradigm of the oppressed in today's world of migrants and displaced persons. But are we bearers of hope? Yes, there's hope through participation.

Simon of Cyrene, himself on a journey from the countryside, and pressed to help Jesus with his cross, evokes participation. Simon reminds us that carrying the cross is a sharing. Matthew 27:32, Mark 15:21, and Luke 23:26–32 narrate the tradition. While Matthew and Mark simply say that Simon carried the cross, Luke personalizes the reference to the cross by adding the words "behind Jesus." He then proceeds to give shape to the scene by adding more context that would further the significance for his mobile and diverse readership.

In reading Luke's additions, we find evident their origin in the psalmic thinking of Israel and Judaism. Even when he does not cite a particular psalm, Luke continues to acknowledge the debt; his New Testament community's understanding of the death and resurrection of Jesus owed much to the Psalter, the biblical collection of psalms. Luke boldly evokes the deepest memories of alienation and repatriation, of praise and lament, of being lost and being found. He does this in a way reminiscent of the prophets. The women of Jerusalem are warned of the difficult judgment awaiting the holy city. "Daughters of Jerusalem," Jesus says, "do not weep for me, but weep for yourselves and for your children" (23:28).

Jerusalem has not known the time of its visitation from God (19:44). The judgment is expressed in the internally contradictive and brutally shocking language of a beatitude: "Blessed are the barren and the wombs that never bore and the breasts that never nursed" (23:29). Luke introduces the beatitude with a dramatic reference to the coming Day of the Lord, writing : "for the days shall come upon you when…" (Luke 19:43 NRSV). This time is often graphically described by the prophets (see Amos 5:18–20, for example), and places us on God's journey. Mountains and hills have experienced the story of Israel's saying both yes and no. The very land itself now joins in the lament and will now be part of the judgment. Hosea declares, and Luke repeats: "They shall say to the mountains, 'Cover us,' and to the hills, 'Fall on us'" (Hos 10:8, Luke 23:30). Lament moves us to see a historical event interpreted as a warning and a challenge, not only to the people of the city but, indeed, to all creation. Nature is called upon by the prophets to testify against Israel in its breach of the covenant. But lament is never God's final word, for the very psalms that supply the language of lament lead us to praise, as in Psalms 22 and 69. All creation groans, notes Paul (Rom 8:19), as it awaits redemption. Because Luke's language is crafted so well, we experience the lament of creation as covenant discourse: "If they do this when the wood is green, what will happen when it is dry?" (23:31).

Thus Luke has woven yet another journey into his vision of Jesus carrying the cross, the journey of creation. Almost every day, we learn something so important that all previous knowledge is instantly put in doubt. A new set of photos from the satellite circling the globe or traveling deep into space fills us with awe. They also testify to our living or not living the claims upon us made by the Creator of All. The person praying the Rosary will be exhilarated to think that the journey to Jerusalem, telescoped into the carrying of the cross, could bear the pilgrimage of humanity in the world as participating in the unfolding of the cosmic journey. Long before Luke worked out these allusions in the years 85 to 90, the Pauline communities had already spoken of the resurrection of Jesus as the new creation and Jesus as its firstborn. Luke's depiction of the way of the cross falls in line with a tradition from the ancient teachers of Israel. Some divined in the mundane folding of a table napkin the struggle to bring order to a chaotic universe, a struggle that still persists for modern science today. The Christian feels in the passage of Rosary beads through his or her fingers the journey within the journey, the spiraling process of contemplating his or her linear history within the task of God to find order and purpose in the midst of randomness.

The psalmist would understand our task, made graceful in the cross of Jesus, of bringing love to bear on this seemingly loveless evolution of the cosmos. There may be difficulty today in claiming that all creation exists for humankind; instead there is a preference to think of humankind as part of the cosmos in its development. Nonetheless, the unique contribution of humankind may not ultimately lie in the gift of intelligence but rather intelligence put at the service of another in love, "the civilization of love," a precept in modern Catholic social teaching. The cross carried by Jesus effectively places before us, not salvation through suffering, but redemption through that love willing to undertake any suffering to overcome the resistance to love. The carrying of the cross is a challenge to the Christian community to live out the particulars of the message of Jesus. Luke is remarkably successful. By the end of the ninth chapter, even before the mission protocol of chapter 10, the journey to Jerusalem in the midst of the ministry shows that love is not an abstraction. Love is concrete, particular, nameable. Rejoice not, Jesus says. In his mission sermon for the disciples after they return from their first experience of preaching, he says, rejoice not that the cosmic powers respond to your preaching (Luke 10:17–20). Rather, rejoice that you share your inheritance through love as did the Samaritan with the Jew, fallen among robbers on the road from Jerusalem to Jericho. There is no contradiction; the cross is no flight from the world but an embrace of the other in caring love and the empowerment of our shared lives.

Luke's multifaceted template engages a contemporary reflection on our life in the twenty-first century. Only love can make it possible for a person to see himself or herself as part of a big cosmic story. For the person who loves, a commitment to space exploration, for example, is also a commitment to the quality of life on this earth. Modern space exploration demands great community involvement, not only within one nation but internationally. The journey is undertaken by a community of sojourners, and the cross condemns any attempt to abuse space for the benefit of the few or the powerful. If we use our new capabilities in space technology against each other, God's creation is mocked, not promoted, by the symbol of the shared cross. Star wars and crosses don't mix; the irresponsibility of the one is ridiculed by the earthiness of the other. Rather than spying on each other's freedom, let satellite technology identify threats against nature—

for example, the danger of a tsunami—and promote creative ways to protect us when nature puts us harm's way.[8]

We are not to go looking for crosses to bear but neither are we to refuse one when it comes. The cross of Jesus is borne in the shape of a neighbor in need, living the gift that we are, as believers, journeying within a shared cosmos, sharing a co-responsibility for a fragile ecosystem, loving in the face of hatred and cruelty, foregoing national hubris to share with all life as gift. The journey of any one human is but a bead in the long rosary of human research and development. Why live as though one were the one and only bead?[9]

†

Fifth Sorrowful Mystery
THE CRUCIFIXION
Matthew 27:33–37, Mark 15:22–26,
Luke 23:26–49, John 19:17–27

"You made known to me the ways of life…"
(Acts 2:28)

What the Star of David is to Israel and the crescent moon to Islam, the cross is to the Christian movement. There is the Protestant cross with no corpus, and the Catholic cross that is always a crucifix. The cruciform, a shape that evokes the memory of a way of killing in the Roman Empire and that was tragically reverted to when a homosexual man was terrorized to death in Wyoming, never fails to repulse. To both the outsider and the insider of the Christian movement, the crucifixion of Jesus remains a source of struggle to identify with and to explain. At least two others, the two thieves, died by crucifixion the day Jesus died. We only remember them because of him. Many others died by crucifixion. So why has the crucifixion of Jesus alone taken on a significance that reaches beyond two millennia? There would be no Christian movement to speak of were it not for the light cast on Jesus' death by the experience of Lord as risen. Notice of his crucifixion, if any at all, would have passed into the annals of history as an interesting detail about execution under Roman imperialism. Such was the treatment of a lawbreaker or an insurrectionist, another example of how Jews were often treated in the Empire.

We Christians have often under-presented the resurrection. Such is the price of the rhetorical skill of the passion narrative, told in all simplicity and modesty. Even the early sermons on the death of Jesus in Acts of the Apostles are gripping in their preaching style (see Acts 3:13–15, 5:30). Yet a contemplation of the crucified could only be sustained on the testimony of those given to know him in his resurrection. "Allowed him to appear" captures well the insight that the religious experience of encounter with the Risen Lord is gift of God (the nuancing of the word *appear* is in Acts 10:40). In light of this gift, we know him, in the power of the resurrection, and in the community of his sufferings (Phil 3:10–11).

Mark is dated around AD 65. Matthew and Luke, using sources available to them, augmented and nuanced Mark's contribution. If Mark were not the first to write down this expression of the community's faith, why would he have left out the additions and nuances of earlier evangelists? This is a good argument for the earliness of Mark's Gospel that in turn sharpens our insights into his priorities in what he had to say. That the early community continued to copy and disseminate Mark shows the profound respect in which he was held. The fact also demonstrates the need of the community to place many templates alongside the template of the received tradition. The contemplation that is at the heart of the practice of the Rosary was already part of the early church's growth in faith. For all, the crucifixion accounts are variations on the story of a man and his profound trust that God would not yield to anyone God's own claim on God's own beloved, a theme already made clear in the very early preaching.

To where, except to their psalms, could the early witnesses take their experience? And there they found the key to interpretation: God did not suffer his faithful one to undergo corruption. Referring to Psalm 16:8–11, Peter's preaching presents all the elements to interpret the experience of the resurrection.

> I saw the Lord always before me,
>> For he is at my right hand so that I will not be shaken;
>> therefore my heart was glad, and my tongue rejoiced;
>> moreover my flesh will live in hope.
> For you will not abandon my soul to live in Hades,
>> or let your Holy One experience corruption.
> You have made known to me the ways of life;
>> you will make me full of gladness with your presence.
>
> (Acts 2:25–28)

How stupendously life-giving is God's claim on his faithful one! When the early community found this voice of faith, it creatively and yet faithfully told the story of the crucifixion. Again we find that each canonical evangelist tells the story, the one story, in the tones of his particular presentation of the Gospel. With no letup, Mark teaches by tragedy. He trusts the Christian reader to draw the connection between Jesus' citation of Psalm 22, "My God, my God, why have you forsaken me," and the testimony of the Roman centurion. "This man was truly God's Son" (Mark 15:34, 39). Mark thus uses what scholars call the messianic secret to withhold revelation, by any human until after the death, of who Jesus really is. The severity of Mark's predeath scene is troubling. The reader recalls the last mention of his disciples, "and all of them deserted him and fled" (14:50), and of Peter, "He broke down and wept" (14:72). In the absence of the disciples, the sarcasm of the chief priests and scribes defines the tragedy: "He saved others; he cannot save himself" (15:31). The system has been saved; another imposter has got his due deserts. Sarcasm yields to irony: "Let the Messiah, the King of Israel, come down from the cross now, so that we may see and believe." If only God would deliver...! "Wait, let us see whether Elijah will come to take him down" (14:36). God fails Jesus, if we judge by our standards. No rescue comes just in the nick of time. All is silent; there's only the watchfulness of the faithful women (15:40). The curtain of the temple is torn in two (15:38). Really, would God abandon his faithful one? Even the women who went to the tomb and found it empty said nothing to anyone for they were afraid (16:9).

Luke brings his deepest feelings as a disciple to bear on the scene. In the cry of Jesus on the cross (23:46), Luke has heard not just the first line of Psalm 22 but the *entire* psalm, in which the complaint of the one who suffers yields to a profound hope that God will answer his or her prayer. Luke sets aside Mark's and Matthew's use of Psalm 22, "My God, my God, why have you forsaken me?" Instead he turns to Psalm 31: "Father, into your hands I commend my spirit." Luke emphasizes the confidence of one who is innocent. This is his testimony, and a foreshadowing of the innocence of the Christian movement in the coming trials. Luke also measures the affect of this testimony on others who are not innocent of the charges laid against them. Totally consistent with the many stories of healing and forgiveness, in the course of his Gospel, Luke presents the scene of the so-called good thief (traditionally, but not biblically, named "Dismas"). The scene between the two thieves is a classic weighing of templates, the situation of the justly accused and that of the innocent Jesus. "Do you not fear God, since you are under the same sentence of condemnation?" asks the good thief. "And we indeed have been condemned justly, for we are getting what we deserve for our deeds, but this man has done nothing wrong" (23:40–41). Jesus' response is a résumé of Luke's Gospel. "Truly I tell you, today you will be with me in Paradise" (v. 43). The language is that of the kingdom. It is highly personalized in the man Jesus. The pardon is immediate, "today." There is no conversion without truth about one's own sinning. There is the affirmation of Jesus' innocence. For many, there is no need of any other detail; this is gospel plain and simple. Even in this dire hour, the pattern is clear. Jesus' first words after he is put on the cross are, "Father, forgive them; for they do not know what they are doing" (23:24). The tradition is shaky at this point for these words are not in all the ancient sources. Even if added by later copyists (but still very early in Christian history), they indicate an intense contemplation of the mind of Luke in presenting Jesus. The prayer of the innocent for forgiveness of those who falsely accuse him is imitable, truly, God's claim upon our lives. Thus Luke anticipates later scenes in the Acts of the Apostles when, before the courts of the empire, the innocence of Jesus of the many charges laid against him applies to the charges against his followers.

All four evangelists note the charge "Jesus, king of the Jews" that is placed on the cross. John explores the chief priests' denial of the title, pointing out that Jesus himself made the claim that he was king of the Jews. Pilate's response, "What I have written, I have written" (19:22), amounts to saying, "Let the chips fall where they may." Pilate exits. The women, whose presence is marked in all the Gospels, appear. They acknowledge in their care for him the claim made upon them by this shepherd king. In John's Gospel, the mother of Jesus, of whom the reader has not heard since the story of Cana, reappears. Her words "Do whatever he tells you" (2:5), first heard at the wedding feast, reverberate in Jesus' commissioning, "Woman, here is your son" (19:26–27). The hour has arrived, the good wine is now, and the claim of Cana is echoed in "Here is your mother…and from that hour the disciple took her into his own home" (19:27). There is joy and profound hope in that simple response of "the disciple whom he loved," (v. 26). Who is the beloved disciple? He or she is the Christian reader who believes that Jesus is the Christ, the son of God, and whom the Risen Lord has embraced in one of the Beatitudes: "Blessed are those who have not seen and yet have come to believe" (20:29, 31) John wrote, he says, that the reader may have life in Jesus' name. Make a decision for Jesus. Let faith in his name be the claim upon you. "Do whatever he tells you" has become a way of life in the world. It contrasts with Pilate's words of disengagement: "I have written what I have written."

That engagement takes many forms and the claim leads one to cross frontiers. All the evangelists seize the story of Joseph of Arimathea to illustrate the point. Mark, as is his wont, gives it to us straight: "Joseph went boldly" (15:43) and asked Pilate for the body of Jesus. John says that Joseph had been a disciple, though secretly for fear of the Jewish leaders (19:38). Luke describes Joseph as a "good and righteous man, who, though a member of the council, had not agreed to their plan and action" (23:50). These are words one would have expected to read in Matthew who presented righteousness as good deeds, but who, perhaps still reeling from the internecine fighting between Jewish and Jewish-Christian synagogues, is at this point satisfied to say simply that Joseph was a disciple. John connects Nicodemus to the adventure of Joseph: "They took the body of Jesus and wrapped it with the spices in linen cloths, according to the burial customs of the Jews" (19:41). In a world where so many bodies are desecrated in mass graves of genocide, which is a word resisted by the powerful to conserve their realpolitik, the story of how the body of Jesus was handled is a reproof of our modern killing fields, and a call to reverence for each human being.

In a church that has accepted belatedly the practice of cremation, there is concern to honor the human person in respecting the human body.[10] This expands to a respect, too, for all creation, because disregard of the body leads to disregard of the world's ecology, and disregard for the world cheapens the meaning of each human being. To live as if we were the last generation flies in the face of the human desire for preservation of the species and mocks the call of God the creator to good stewardship of the earth and cosmos. The body begs transformation for life with God for all eternity. We will always be body, fashioned in one way for life here, fashioned in another for life there. We cannot *not* be body. As water oozed out of the earth and gave God the artist the wherewithal to form humankind (Gen 2:7), likewise on the cross of Jesus, blood and water flowed from his pierced side (19:34), and humankind is reclaimed. John illuminates his presentation with biblical references to the paschal lamb whose bones would not be broken (19:36–37). In the image of water flowing from the side of Christ, he brings full circle a literary symbolism let loose in the scene at the feast of dedication of his visit to Jerusalem (7:37). As the cadaver of Jesus grew cold on the lap of his mother, our eternal pieta, John pried open the Christian imagination to a world reclaimed in the missionary body of Christ.

Like any body, Jesus' body is the receiver and giver of life. Jesus is the good shepherd who has laid down his life that we may have life. Looking on the pierced side of Jesus, Christians have seen and felt a heart of intense and immense love, indefatigably there that we and "the other sheep" may have life in the communion that Jesus shared with the Father. How many a mother like Mary has received into her arms the broken body of her child and looked for conviction that the death of her child could mean life and renewal for others? In the deepest emotions that touch us in such a vision, so often repeated in our world today, God's claim upon us is irresistibly presented. The risen body of Jesus is no cadaver, but a body of action, missionary and outreaching, a community expressing itself in a passion for humanity. May nothing lessen the poignancy of John's vision of Jesus' final gift of blood and water on the cross, but may all life's experiences ask us to dare to become that body, broken and raised, for others.

3

THE GLORIOUS MYSTERIES

†

First Glorious Mystery
JESUS IS RAISED
Matthew 28, Mark 16, Luke 24, and John 20

"...the one who raised the Lord Jesus will raise us also..."
(2 Cor 4:14)

Here's the nub of our faith: God raised Jesus from the dead and "showed him off" to the disciples. The resurrection of Jesus has primarily to do with the God of the resurrection, and Jesus would not have understood it otherwise. Who is this God of the living who lays claim to the whole of creation? Often we ask, Did Jesus know that he would be raised? The answer is no, Jesus did not know, but he trusted completely in the God of his ancestors, the God who was faithful to Israel, the God who keeps promises, the God of the covenant, the God about whom Jesus' mother sang in profound trust. Jesus learned from Mary's and Joseph's Judaism to trust God! Because the Gospels were written in the light of the resurrection and the experience of the Risen Lord in the communities of faith and worship, any scene from any one of the Gospels or any part of the New Testament can be viewed as a celebration of faith in the God who raised Jesus from the dead.

Resurrection is not resuscitation, the mere revival to this life, even if resuscitation is the image we most often use. In the story of the woman married to seven brothers (Luke 20:27–40 and parallels), we see an example of how the New Testament handled the ridicule that comes with presenting resurrection as resuscitation. Paul's discussion in 1 Corinthians shows that there were, from the beginning, other ways to put into words the central belief. He writes:

> but in fact Christ has been raised from the dead, the first fruits of those who have died....Christ the first fruits, then at his coming those who belong to Christ. Then comes the end when he hands over the kingdom to God the Father, after he has destroyed every ruler and every authority and power. (1 Cor 15:20, 23–24)

This text offers us a great framework, built around kingdom as claim, within which to interpret the experience. As Son, Jesus surrendered to the Father the kingdom to which he has subjected all things. "The Son," the text goes on to say, "will himself be subject in his turn to the One who subjected all things to him so that God may be all in all" (28).

Easter faith is a celebration of the God disclosed as the Father of Jesus of Nazareth and giver of the Spirit in whom Jesus is experienced as wrapped up in God for all time. The resurrection is the ultimate expression of kingdom as claim. It is the symbol of God's claim upon Jesus as Son and on us as adopted sons and daughters. As obedient Son, Jesus surrenders to the claim of God upon himself and in him, God's claim upon all of us.

At this point we are reading some early expressions of the community's developing Easter faith. Still within the Corinthian correspondence, we read, "We too believe…knowing that he who raised the Lord Jesus to life will raise us with Jesus in our turn" (2 Cor 4:13). This passage comes within a major development of faith in the Risen Lord, on whose face shines the same light that God shone into darkness when God created the world. In time (and still within Paul), there are other formulations that place the act of raising Jesus from the dead within the work of God as tri-une: "If the Spirit of him who raised Jesus from the dead is living in you, then he who raised Jesus from the dead will give life to your mortal bodies through his Spirit living in you" (Rom 8:11; see also 2 Cor 4:14).

I always marvel that these reflections from Paul on living the resurrection faith preceded the drawing together of the stories of the experience of the Risen Lord in the Gospels. Knowing this helps me to appreciate that the evangelists had much material from which to select. John says as much in the closing verses of his Gospel (21:25). He thereby invites a Christian reader, in appreciating the selection made, to bring his or her lived experience of paschal faith to bear on the telling. In this way, we participate in the proclamation. Alongside the well-tailored telling by each evangelist to complete the respective Gospel, in Matthew 28, Mark 16, and especially Luke 24, there were pastiches of texts such as we have in the longer ending of Mark (16:9–16) and in the additions to First Corinthians (15:1–11). Carefully constructed, these selections work because the texts were written for communities already long practiced in contemplation of their new condition through faith in Jesus the Risen Lord. The texts were accepted as gospel because they faithfully reflected the faith of the respective communities. Every word and every image would have evoked a response of an affirming "Amen." Thus the communities fulfilled the several goals of proclamation, sound teaching, and apology.

In honoring the apologetic concerns of his gospel presentation, Matthew masterfully inspired a sense of confidence. He interjected references to the guard at the tomb within stories of the burial, appearances, and commissioning. This deployment of Roman guards, requested by the Jewish authorities (27:62–63) could not suppress the good news of the resurrection. Thus we have the following pattern: Jesus (27:57–61), guard (vv. 62–66), Jesus (2:1–10), guard (vv. 11–15), and Jesus (vv. 16–20). This pattern recalls a similar arrangement at the opening of Matthew's narrative.[1] Herod's attempts to kill the Messiah were futile against the dreams of Joseph: Joseph (1:18–25), Herod (2:1–12), Joseph (vv. 13–19), Herod (vv. 16–18), and Joseph (vv. 19–23). With all opposition now overcome, the commissioning with which the narrative ends (28:16–20) is all the more powerful. Jesus, whom the disciples worship now as Risen Lord, in words from Daniel the prophet, claimed, "All authority on heaven and on earth has been given to me" (28:19), and then Jesus commanded, "Go, therefore, and make disciples of all nations; baptizing them in the name of the Father and of the Son and of the Holy Spirit." The Father through the Risen Lord in the church's mission continues to lay claim in the Spirit on all creation and all peoples. This is a most suitable ending to Matthew's narrative portrait of Jesus, written as a sure guide for a community in an epoch-making transition between synagogue and church. It is also a foundational expression of the paschal faith that can be traced in all the New Testament assertions: the Father raises Jesus the Son and sends the Holy Spirit.

Luke upholds this foundational Christian assertion in how he arranges his stories in chapter 24 around the disclosure of the Risen Lord to the disciples on the road to Emmaus (24:13–35). The homily of Jesus is a gospel within a gospel, and the necessity of the suffering and death of the Messiah now surrenders to the injunction to go to the city and to await the promise of the Father, the Spirit! "So stay here in the city until you have been clothed with power from on high" (24:49). Jesus, in Luke, asks the disciples to return to Jerusalem to await the gift of the Spirit. Luke here puts into narrative form the triune foundational formula of faith expressed by Paul in Romans 8:11: "If the Spirit of him who raised Jesus from the dead dwells in you, he who raised Christ from the dead will give life to your mortal bodies also through his Spirit that dwells in you." Note in particular Paul's reference to the Spirit as "of him who raised…" and Luke's presentation of the Spirit as "what my Father promised." The power commissioning the community in Matthew 28:16–20 is the same empowerment that underlies the opening scenes of Luke's second volume. There, Luke will begin with the question of when the kingdom is to be restored. Under the umbrella of that question, he carries the commissioning of the Risen Lord, in the promise of the Spirit, from Jerusalem to Rome, the very center of the Empire. In an abundance of joy, the Christian reader goes from text to text to treasure the inexhaustible riches of this new found faith.[2]

Easter faith is mission. As in our Easter liturgy, we no sooner celebrate the Risen Lord than we ask what does this mean for the world? And here Luke is forthright and clear: forgiveness! "Repentance and forgiveness of sins is to be proclaimed in his name to all nations" (Luke 24:47). John's presentation of the Risen Lord also concerns the power to forgive sin (and the gift of peace) given to the assembled church (John 20:19–23). In raising Jesus from the dead, God delivered on the new imagination for life in this world opened up by Jesus' preaching of the kingdom. The evangelists are one in presenting paschal faith as action in the world, at once deeply personalized and yet wider and greater than any one individual. In juxtaposing Peter and the disciple whom Jesus loved, we have both the personalized response in the disciple whom Jesus loved and the inauguration of the community in Peter that is greater than any one individual: feed my lambs, feed my sheep (21:15–17).[3]

The story of Mary of Magdala (John 20:11–18) dramatizes this duality: she has a deeply personal connection with Jesus ("Rabboni") and a mission to the disciples ("Go to my brothers"). She is also forever freed from a nostalgia for the old days ("Do not hold onto me," John 20:17) by which the church is permitted to trust the Spirit as the community moves into new places and new times.[4] Jesus says, "I am ascending to my Father and your Father, to my God and your God" (20:17). In these words, he recalls his final discourse: "As you [Father] have sent me into the world, so I have sent them into the world" (17:18).

The template of the person praying this mystery of the Rosary is the template of the early Christians joyfully relishing this sharing of witness to the Risen Lord. The resurrection is not the final proof that Jesus is divine, and these stories are not intended to prove anything. The community comes to these texts already gifted in faith and wanting to celebrate and deepen their grasp of this earth-shattering and kingdom-building outpouring of power and love, of forgiveness and acceptance, of peace and newfound solidarity of all humankind. The texts legitimate the experience of the Risen Lord in the liturgy of the assembled communities. The story of Emmaus jumps off the page for the community that knows what it is to celebrate the presence to them, with them, and for them of the Risen Lord, just as Israel rejoiced and praised God in the temple for the presence to, with, and for them of the God of their ancestors. Awash in tears for the joy of Mary of Magdala, known since as "the apostle to the apostles," the community is rejoicing in the apostolicity of their gift of faith and its succession in faith-filled witnesses. The Rosary "pray-er" will come to know that this mystery of the resurrection is without limits. Although four more mysteries of the Rosary will still be too little to express the swelling joy, the only reason the text works is because of what we ourselves bring, our God-bestowed hope: "Deep calls to deep / at the thunder of your cataracts; / all your waves and your billows / have gone over me.... / Hope in God; for I shall again praise him, / my help and my God!" (Ps 42:7, 11b) Alleluia!

†

Second Glorious Mystery
JESUS' ASCENSION
Acts 1:6–12, Ephesians 4:7–8

"He made captivity itself a captive;..."
(Eph 4:8)

Luke is outstanding among New Testament writers in developing the theme of the ascension of Jesus. But he is not alone in presenting the event, and the reader can encounter elements of his presentation in the other sources. However, in all the New

Testament references, it is possible to notice a missionary interpretation. Matthew (28:16–20) emphasizes the journey to Galilee mentioned earlier: "And indeed he is going ahead of you to Galilee" (28:7; see also Mark 16:7). Earlier in the story, the evangelists had established Galilee as a symbol of missionary activity. For instance, Matthew himself, in introducing the ministry of Jesus (4:15), gives a distinctly missionary thrust to "Galilee of the Gentiles" in his quotation of Isaiah 8:23. In chapter 28, Matthew notes Galilee but does not name the mountain (of the ascension?) to which the disciples were directed: "The eleven disciples went to Galilee to the mountain to which Jesus had directed them"(28:16). However, within the entire scene of 28:16–20, Matthew evokes the missionary exaltation of Jesus, thinking of the passage in Daniel 7:14, where one like the Son of Man, coming on the clouds, is given all dominion, glory, and kingship. In the longer ending of Mark (16:9–20), the text says clearly that the Lord Jesus was taken up into heaven and sat down at the right hand of God. By the time of this addition to Mark, the tradition had solidified around an image of Jesus' ascension and expanded into images of exaltation: that is, sitting at the right hand of God. Although the name *Galilee* does not appear in the addition to Mark, the missionary thrust is honored with mention of the extraordinary gifts being given to the missionaries.

In John's Gospel, Jesus discloses to Mary of Magdala that he is ascending (20:17). The reader is not unprepared. In fact, in an earlier chapter (12:32), we read the words of Jesus: "I, when *I am lifted up* from the earth, will draw all people to myself" (emphasis added). Commentaries on John's Gospel call attention to an ambiguity: is the reference here to lifting up on the cross, or being assumed into heaven?[5] The question is important because it invites us to consider the biblical images *ascension* and *assumption* as distinct responses of God to the suffering and death of Jesus. Assumption is usually denoted in the passive voice (for example, "has been taken up" Acts 1:11), and this is seen as reference to the action of God. Generally, that fits better with the usual image of the plan of salvation that God raised Jesus and took him up. I will discuss more about this when we come to the mystery of the assumption of Mary. There, the nuances can be more sharply described because there is no discussion of Mary either raising herself or of ascending. As we will see, her life is said to be altogether wrapped up in God by God! That's the primordial point about Jesus in 1 Corinthians 15:28: "When all things are subjected to him, then the Son himself will also be subjected to the one who put all things in subjection under him, so that God may be all in all."

Luke chose to take ascension, the traditional way of speaking about God's response to the death of Jesus, and to develop it by building in a period of time between Passover and Pentecost, and setting the ascension a few days before the outpouring of the Spirit.[6] How Luke ends his Gospel indicates that he had already chosen how he would open his second volume.

> Then he led them out as far as Bethany, and lifting his hands, he blessed them. While he was blessing them, he withdrew from them and was carried up into heaven. And they worshipped him, and returned to Jerusalem with great joy; and they were continually in the temple blessing God. (24:50–53)

What genius for Luke to get so many of his favorite themes mentioned in this closing scene of the Gospel and yet whet the appetite for more to come! The Christian reader notes that Luke strategically awaits Acts 1:11 and there reuses his favorite words for the assumption: "this Jesus who has been taken up." Luke already used the phrase in 9:51: "when the days drew near for him to be taken up." At that crucial turning point in the plot (9:51), Jesus "set his face" to go to Jerusalem. For Luke, Jesus' life is one journey to Jerusalem and, indeed, through Jerusalem not only to Rome in the person of the missionary community but to the right hand of God where Stephen will see him in glory (Acts 7:55). Luke then focuses the attention of the Christian reader on the disciples, having come back to Jerusalem to await the gift of the Father. Jesus calls the disciples to a persuasive participation: "I am sending upon you what my Father promised; so stay in the city until you are clothed with power from on high" (Luke 24:49). The rhetoric is perfect. Luke has found a way to dramatize what Matthew promises in the words of Jesus, the ever-present rabbi: "I am with you always, to the end of the age" (Matt 28:20). The assurance that the Risen Lord watches over and guides the community of the church is an assurance as much needed in today's broken world as then. The ascension of Jesus functions like the invitation of the Song of Songs: "He brought me to the banqueting house, / and his intention toward me was love" (2:4).

This assurance of the Risen Lord to the community is key to the lectionary readings for the feast of the ascension. There, the praying church reads the Letter to the Ephesians: "But each of us was given grace according to the measure of Christ's gift. Therefore, it is said, / 'When he ascended on high he made captivity captive; / he gave gifts to his people'" (4:7–8). The citation is from Psalm 68:19. But does Paul's citation of the psalm mean anything more than he was looking for a text that spoke of gifts, the topic under discussion? Did Paul cite more than he needed? Or is there a relationship between the gifts received in Christ for which Paul has just offered a wonderful prayer of thanksgiving (3:14–21) and the theme of ascending to take captivity captive? Yes, there is a relationship. Our discussion of that connection between gifts and ascension will involve us in a reflection on Paul's use of christological hymns, conversion as a world-altering experience in which we are sustained by Jesus' ascension and exaltation, and the place of the community in which brothers and sisters are gifts. (See Ephesians 4:11–16.)

Psalm 68 is a marvelous psalm singing the praises of God, who "rides upon the clouds" (v. 5), and enters into cosmic battles on behalf of his people. "You ascended the high mount, / leading captives in your train, / and receiving gifts from people, / even from people who rebel against the Lord God's dwelling there" (v. 18). Later, in verses 32–33, we read: "Sing to God, O kingdoms of the earth; / sing praises to the Lord, / O rider in heavens, the ancient heavens." In reinterpreting Psalm 68, Paul is presenting the victorious God as giving gifts: that is, giving gifted brothers and sisters to the community. But the gifts are not only for the community in itself but for the mission of the community "to make everyone see what is the plan of the mystery hidden for ages in God who created all things" (Eph 3:9). This is then expanded and explained: "So that through the church the wisdom of God in its rich variety might now be made known to the rulers and authorities in the heavenly places" (3:10).

The interplay of the reference to ascending in Ephesians 4:8–10 with the earlier exaltation theme in 1:15–23 enriches the ascension imagery. Note especially verses 20 and 21: "God put this power to work in Christ when he raised him from the dead and seated him at his right hand in the heavenly places, far above all rule and authority and power and dominion, and above every name that is named, not only in this age but also in the age to come." Paul is giving thanks because the newly converted

Ephesians are grasping the implications of faith in Christ, whose ascended and exalted status shapes their life in this world. He prays further that they will be enlightened to know the power that God has worked in Christ by raising him from the dead.

What makes reference in Ephesians all the more exciting is that Paul is not citing Psalm 68 to develop explicitly the cosmic or ecological aspect of Christian faith. In Ephesians, Paul is more concerned for the relationship of Jew and Gentiles and the proper comportment of the Christian. The same is true of the christological hymn in Paul's Letter to the Philippians (2:5–11). There he is speaking of the Christian character of humbly living with others. That hymn recalls the self-emptying *(kenosis)* of the one "in the form of God," the suffering and the taking on of the form of a slave even to death, death on a cross. God exalted him "and gave him the name / that is above every name, / that at the name of Jesus / every name should bend, / in heaven and on earth and under the earth" (2:10). The allusion to those in heaven and on earth and under the earth is not as expansive as "all rule and authority and power and dominion and every name that is named not only in this age but also in the one to come" in the text of Ephesians, but the same connection between life here in the Christian community and life in the cosmos is evident.

The reader will note, too, that in the use of a christological hymn in the Letter to the Colossians, the writer expresses his concern about the difficulty of living the new faith in the place of the old: "See to it that no one takes you captive through philosophy and empty deceit, according to human tradition, according to the elemental spirits of the universe, and not according to Christ" (2:8). Paul is working pastorally in situations where these aspects of faith in Jesus Christ are being intensely discussed. This is

exhortation, to which the Hellenists ascribed a certain nonnego-
tiable character by the use of the word *parenesis*. This word carries
an "in your face," incontrovertible but not unreasoning, presentation of what faith in Christ means for life in this world.

Does all this come together? Even before the Gospels were
written, the Christian community had already found ways to
focus on the resurrection of Jesus in the symbols of assumption
and enthronement. The image of resuscitation to this life was
useful, but it was limited and perhaps too vulnerable to misunder-
standing. The Gospels therefore presented Jesus, the Risen Lord,
in terms of resurrection, ascension, and exaltation. In the ascension, a sense of mission, already present in the resurrection stories,
is renewed. Paul's discussion develops that missionary sense, giving it a more cosmic significance, now necessary because of the
difficulty of conversion. Conversion, as the engagement of the
whole person, Paul learned early, is a matter of reimagining one's
symbolic world. Beyond the proclamation of the kingdom and the
acceptance of baptism, the harder part of the conversion process
was building the images necessary to make the newfound faith in
Jesus commensurate to, and even more compelling than, the old
mythologies and symbolic structures. The claim made on the person had to be worked out in the context of many counter-claims.
"See to it that no one takes you captive," to cite again the words of
the writer of the Letter to the Colossians (2:8), "through philosophy
and empty deceit, according to human tradition, according to the
elemental spirits of the universe, and not according to Christ."

Are we overloading the symbol of ascension at this point?
How do the early Christian hymns, celebrating ascension and
exaltation, relate to, and draw from, the claim imposed on us in
Jesus' proclamation of the reign of God? We are invited to take a

second look. Christians involved in the RCIA process know this struggle when it comes to presenting a Catholic-Christian ethos to new converts. The difficult part of postbaptismal instruction (mystagogy) is getting us to accept the vocation to be Catholic: that is, to internalize the radically inclusive claim of Christian faith. That inclusive claim today is nothing less than cosmological and involves us in stewardship of the universe.

Contemporary science opens up many new avenues of understanding the universe. The early church—in probing the meaning of the resurrection of the "image of the invisible God, the firstborn of all creation" (Col 1:15)—had already intuited an appreciation of these new avenues. There is nothing, according to Christian faith, that will ever be discovered by science that has not already been grasped as belonging to the capture that Jesus Christ made of all creation. The one who rides the clouds has taken hold of the movement from chaos to order, big bang theory included! Ephesians 4:9–10 reads: "When it says 'He ascended,' what does it mean but that he had also descended into the lower parts of the earth? He who descended is the same one who ascended far above all the heavens, so that he might fill all things." Obviously, the wording is itself chaotic because Paul is trying his hand at what we today call intertextual reading. He is reworking Psalm 68 and bringing the faith of the Christian into dialogue with all the deep reflection that once gave the mythologies expression in that psalm. But the Christian message gets through; the victory of God over chaos finds its newest and most purposeful expression in Jesus whose goal is to lead all in a victory celebration to God the creator of all! It is for participation in that victory that God has given gifts to us.

The template of the one praying the Rosary is never unaffected by the place we hold in God's creation. We are not outside nature; we are ourselves nature, one with all creation, using our gift of intelligence, hopefully not to dominate but to take our place within nature. Everything we know, we learn from nature. In allowing nature to teach us, we are allowing nature's claim upon us. In learning from the earth how to farm, from the seas how to fish, from the earth how to mine, from the body how to heal, and from space how to travel, are we not enwrapped in the deepest lessons the human family draws from nature?

Christian faith sees this fact confirmed, over and over again, by the wisdom tradition in scriptures and, especially, in the sage preaching of Jesus. Faith and science are dealing with the same reality, nature.[7] Faith and science complement one another in searching for the appropriate skills to handle nature, and for the appropriate mythological language with which to celebrate nature and to hold ourselves in awe at so wondrous a gift. The Christian knows that in Jesus' resurrection and the ascension, he did not undo his condition as one of us. At one point in history, some Christians claimed that Jesus was no longer human when he was raised. It's not so. In fact, he embraced our condition all the more, and his ascension expands our minds to where our knowledge of nature can lead us. He took our pride and our shortsightedness captive, so that in place of spoiling nature of its innate capacity to lead us to rapturous heights, we would use our gifts to constantly improve ways to live our human dignity here as brothers and sisters. The gifts of nature are for all, not the few who are rich. Nature is to be used, not abused, and to be explored for the benefit of all humankind, not its detriment, and never for the destruction of the human family.

An integrated view is never just opening the new frontier of knowledge but the responsible use of that knowledge for the good of all. The ever-widening divide between the haves and the have-nots in today's globalized economy is a direct affront to the meaning of the ascension that celebrates Christ's capture of the forces of greed and maximum profit. The ascension moves us to look at the development of the whole human family. Jesus' aim is not the fullness of some but the fullness of all (Eph 4:10). One could expand this reflection into the biblical images of *pleroma* and *apokatastatis*, the first speaking to the fullness of the re-creation act in Christ (Eph 1:23), and the latter to the sense of restoration of all things in Christ (Acts 3:21). This comprehension of the significance of the death and resurrection of Jesus comes to us through the ascension, with the divine distribution of gifts and the taking captive of contrary forces: the inevitable counter-claims.

When we Christians celebrate the ascension we are not saying that everything is accomplished; we are saying that in Christ there is a way opened, and where he has gone, we are to follow. In the Preface for the feast of the ascension we pray, "Christ has passed beyond our sight, not to abandon us but to be our hope. He is the beginning, the head of the church; where he has gone, we hope to follow." Ascension is not disengagement; it is design, discipleship, and mission. It is not the task of the ascended one to give us a timetable but to give us the Spirit. "Lord, is this the time when you will restore the kingdom to Israel?" the disciples ask (Acts 1:6). Jesus responds:

> "It is not for you to know the times or periods that the Father has set by his own authority. But you will receive power when the Holy Spirit has come upon you; and you will be my witnesses in Jerusalem, in all Judea and Samaria, and to the ends of the earth." (Acts 1:7–8)

Many aspects arise when we contemplate the ascension, and so the Rosary devotee looks forward in time to the Mystery of the Assumption of Mary to ponder more deeply the real meaning of Jesus' ascension for our daily lives. "Why do you stand looking up toward heaven?" ask the two men dressed in white garments (Acts 1:11). The two, whose presence recalls the morning of the resurrection (Luke 24:4), tell us that in the ascension we are celebrating a variation on the resurrection theme. They assure the disciples: "This Jesus, who has been taken up from you into heaven, will come in the same way as you saw him go into heaven" (Acts 1:11). In the meantime, we are learning that Christian hope is always tied to a person risen, glorified, and ascended, and more intimately present to us than in his historically and socially limited days.

†

Third Glorious Mystery
THE SPIRIT AS GIFT OF THE RISEN LORD
Acts 2:1–4, 17–21; 17:6

**"These people who have been turning
the world upside down..."**
(Acts 17:6)

The Christian praying the Rosary comes to this mystery as if returning home! Were it not for the gift of the Spirit, we would not be praying the Rosary. That simple statement gives rise to a desire to go to all the places in scripture where such a statement is justified. Paul, for example, says that no one can say, "Jesus is

Lord" except by the Spirit (1 Cor 12:3). In another place, Paul claims that the Spirit cotestifies with our spirit that we are the children of God (Rom 8:16). First Corinthians 12 and Romans 8, both Pauline texts, suggest the ways in which God claims us. Integral to the claim is the gift of the Spirit.

Claim is the word that I have used to describe the kingdom or reign of God that Jesus announced. With the experience of the Risen Lord, the claim of the kingdom is the gift of the Spirit. A thorough study of Paul would show the linkage between the Spirit and the kingdom because both are images of God's "making me his own" in the experience of the Risen Lord (see Phil 3:12, literally "grasping me."). As believers, we are engaged in such a way that we cannot turn away. That summons on everything we are is experienced as the gift of the Spirit. Paul had his own way of stating this claim upon us: "If I proclaim the gospel, this gives me no ground for boasting, for an obligation is laid on me and woe to me if I do not proclaim the gospel!" (1 Cor 9:16).

So, in turning to this mystery of Pentecost, the Rosary devotee is at home in the Spirit and finds his or her spirit witnessing, together with the very Spirit of God, that we are the children of God. Christians are coheirs of the inheritance of which the Spirit is the first installment (see Eph 1:14). Before exploring some of this imagery, it is important to give another reason why the person praying the Rosary is on familial territory. Mary, the mother of Jesus, is among the disciples awaiting the gift of the Father from on high (Acts 1:14, Luke 24:49). Luke is not unlike John. The fourth evangelist, once having introduced the mother of Jesus into the narrative at the wedding feast of Cana, returns to her in the special hour of Jesus. Luke, once having developed the place of Mary within the story, does not forget her at the beginning of the Book of Acts when Mary has a special gift to offer to the new community. She is the person, in the story as told by Luke, who is prepared to teach the disciples how to live in the Spirit. In Mary, spirit and word come together. She hears God's word and keeps it. Luke presents this way to appreciate her virginal conception of Jesus: The angel says to her, "The Holy Spirit will come upon you" (1:35). Elizabeth then salutes Mary as "blessed is she who believed that there would be a fulfillment of what was spoken to her by the Lord" (1:45). Later, a woman in the crowd cries out to Jesus, "Blessed is the womb that bore you and the breasts that nursed you," and he answers, "Blessed are those who hear the word of God and obey it" (11:27–28). Living with such trust in God's fidelity, as will become apparent in our contemplation of the joyful mysteries, is Mary's template of life in the Spirit. That's her great lesson of living with the reversal of our human expectation.

The Christian, then, comes to the contemplation of Pentecost out of the experience of the Spirit. Who can doubt that Luke's own dramatic presentation of Pentecost is itself the fruit of the gift of the Spirit given to him to be an evangelist? His skills come together to shape the image of the Spirit that has shaped the Christian movement. Ask yourself how often you have seen paintings of Pentecost and listened to homilies and explanations about Pentecost. While many times good or even brilliant, do they not fall short of Luke's dramatic unfolding? Luke will describe the Pentecost event with his regular attentiveness to historical, social, and even political concerns. Luke will give an array of rereadings of the psalms and prophets to bolster his religious message. As he draws on many sources, Luke rightly assumed that his reader would enjoy his literary ingenuity in rendering the scene of a Pentecost celebration in Jerusalem. Jews came from across the whole world to celebrate and pray in the variety of synagogues. These represented the many different places of the Jewish diaspora and the different languages spoken. For many, to go to Jerusalem was a once-in-a-lifetime experience. Knowing all this, Luke captures, within the excitement of what was usual for such an occasion, what was unusual about this particular event: the year that Jesus of Nazareth died.

The one reality that Luke wants the Christian reader to bring to the text is his or her experience of the Spirit. Here, in depending on the response of the Christian reader, Luke is like John who, in Jesus' beatitude to Thomas, characterizes all modern readers: "Blessed are those who have not seen and yet have come to believe" (20:29). That's us today. To repeat what Paul said: No one confesses Jesus as Lord except in the Spirit. In bringing our experience of the Spirit to bear on the text of the Pentecost event, we enter today into the testimony of the Spirit that we are sons and daughters of God. Luke, in his presentation of the affective response of the community, illustrates this testimony (Acts 1:13–14, 2:42–47, 4:23–37). These passages are known as summary passages; they review the narrative action that has taken place and help to shape the readers' affective response. If John salutes us in anticipation of our faith (John 20:29), Luke appeals to us on the basis of our lived experience of the Spirit.

In contemplating Pentecost, the Christian comes out of the energy and love of the Trinity: the Spirit of the One who raised Jesus Christ. In reading about the people who had come from the various parts of the Jewish world to celebrate the giving of the Torah in the Feast of Pentecost, the Christian is put in touch with the very foundation of our faith in Jesus the Messiah: the covenant made with David (Acts 2:1–36), and the blessing given to

Abraham that all the nations of the world would be blessed in him (3:25–26). The language of the Spirit is understood by all because the great wind that blew over the chaos at the dawn of creation is now given a name and is the gift of a very memorable and holy man now raised in glory! Whereas diversity was once interpreted as God's punishment for pride, as in the story of Babel in Genesis 11, now diversity is seen as reason to give praise and glory to God as in Acts 2:14–47. The Christian finds a new energy to face down all fear, even the fear of ridicule, of marginalization, even of persecution and martyrdom. We read the story of people, once timid and fearful, now bold and willing to confess their faith (4:13). Only in the Spirit, who gives gifts to all, is there the room to accept all and to rejoice in each other's gifts. The diversity is astounding: international, intercultural, and intergenerational. Luke turns in Acts 2:17 to Joel 3:1 to help paint the scene: "Your sons and your daughters shall prophesy, / and your young men shall see visions, / and your old men shall dream dreams!"

The contemplation of Pentecost doesn't end with the closing of that great day. The movement, made up of people confessing faith in Jesus Christ, is a movement of the Spirit. This Spirit testifies to the brothers and sisters in many and diverse situations: in their communities, at the gate of the temple, in a chariot riding home to Ethiopia, in civic court and palaces, in health care, in the circle of the learned scientists and philosophers of the day, increasingly in prisons, vividly in the presence of the broken and the pushed-aside, and at no point more dramatically than in the call of Paul and the conversion of the shortsightedness of Peter to include the Gentiles.

The Christians were accused of turning the world upside down (Acts 17:6). It's a great indictment! And if there is anyone who would enjoy the accusation, it is Mary. She knew the power of the Spirit and taught the church to live in the Spirit who turns the world upside down. Already in Luke's first volume, as Jesus makes his way to Jerusalem (9:51—19:44), he too turns the world upside down, gathering in all the wrong people. Thus, Jesus lavishly portrays God as forgiving and reconciling (chapter 15). This way of challenging our expectations, indeed, our comforts, continues in the story of Acts of the Apostles. The stories are only examples of what might be called the inauguration speeches of Jesus and Mary. Each speaker is filled with the power of the Spirit. Jesus, in his homily in the synagogue in Nazareth (Luke 4:14–18), and Mary, in her manifesto in the Magnificat (1:35–47), are really offering mission statements. Thus Luke puts Christians in touch with the summons of the kingdom, the claim of the Spirit that gives birth to the church. All is claim and all is gift, not our accomplishments. Mary, who learned to trust the Spirit and sought out Spirit-led people to help her discern her call in life, is a model of humility: "Here I am, the servant of the Lord; let it be with me according to your word" (Luke 1:38). This is the only template that makes sense in lives lived in the Spirit. This is a stinging rebuke to the little pomposities with which we often do the work of Jesus, who, though being equal to God, set aside being God and took the form of a slave (Phil 2:5–11). "What do you have that you did not receive?" asks Paul, who then answers his own question, "But if you received it, why do you boast as if it were not a gift?" (1 Cor 4:7).

Setting the template of these revolutionary passages over against the template of our lived experience could fill the person praying the Rosary with a certain agitation, a certain anger that we as Christians have so domesticated the gospel of Jesus that little of the fire of Pentecost gets through.[8] In the post–Vatican II church

113

there was a reawakening to the power and the testimony of the Spirit. I leave to others to analyze why the charismatic movement in the church was not developed and nurtured, but not before I thank God for the many wonderful awakenings that came with the movement. I recall giving a pre-Pentecost retreat in a suburban church in Penfield, New York. Night after night, the church was filled with brothers and sisters wanting to praise God and give glory for the outpouring of the Spirit. Many who experienced this new outpouring, on their own testimony, left behind dry, spiritless days of churchgoing. They wanted more than just a moralized Christian life of do's and don'ts. For many the words of Ezekiel (37:1–14) were realized: the Spirit was being poured out on dry bones. At prayer gatherings in Potomac, Maryland, I accompanied a person with cerebral palsy who for the first time spoke in church and praised God loudly and joyously. Apart from the exaggerations of a few and the reservations of some others, no one was claiming that the gift of the Spirit was a new experience, but that the church was newly aware to what the life of the community may truly be, life in "the Spirit of him who raised Jesus from the dead," as Paul most beautifully places before us the economy of God's ways with humankind and all creation (Rom 8:11).

The mystery of Pentecost puts the person praying the Rosary in touch with our giftedness as claim. Everyone's gifts come to life in the power of the Spirit. There are gifts of the Spirit, but the Spirit is the one who gives recognition and purpose and direction to the exercise of the gifts already within us. It is when the gifts of the Spirit make contact with these gifts that we then can speak of the co-testimony that the Spirit gives to our spirit. In the awakening of our skills and the realization that others stand in need of the skills we have, we experience a new purpose, a new sense of mission. Paul tells us to rejoice in the diversity of gifts, at times the most common of gifts. We are to be alive to the needs of our brothers and sisters in sharing these simple gifts. The issue is not the particular gift but the love with which we lay our gift at the service of our neighbor. At times, if the love of our brother or sister demands it in a particular setting, we are called to the surrender of our gift; for example, stifling a desire to finish another's sentence because you already intuit where an argument is headed. Our life is not our own, our gifts are not our own. They find their deepest meaning as celebrations of the love with which we have been loved and the knowledge with which we have been known (1 Cor 8:2–3, 13:12–13).

The mystery of Pentecost is the mystery of gifts received and gifts given in love. Often we think that if a skill is a gift of God, it must be a joy to share. Perhaps in retrospect, it may be a joy, but in the time of giving, it is often a thorn in our side, an angel of Satan to buffet us and make life hard and difficult. Not all gifts are easy to live with, and we would prefer not having them. Many are blessed with a gift of insight and can instantly tell insincerity and deceit. Many are blessed with a thirst for justice and the capacity to stand alongside the poor in our struggle for a more just world. The gifts of the prophets led to their being thrown out of the community, to their sitting in stinking urban water wells, to being considered a fringe element in their own society, or ultimately to their being martyred. What the Bible teaches about a community of prophets witnessing over generations is often true of us. One's gifts are carried as part of the heritage of the community, and their deepest meaning is often only discerned in retrospect. Often we travel in blindness; only later times will show that the gift was prophetic and led the community on the right path. How often have the insights of theologians and peace-and-justice activists been repudiated and put down in their own time, then vindicated later? One gifted by God lives the truth and asks not to be vindicated within one's own lifetime. Jesus remains for us the gifted one who died shamefully but innocent. The experience of the Risen Lord, Giver of the Holy Spirit, vindicates, and makes even more relevant now, Jesus' message and purpose. If only in the Spirit can one confess Jesus is Lord, then only in the Spirit can one endure the rejection of one's gifts in the present with hope that all will be worked out in God's plan. In a deep reflection on some painful experiences, Paul not only speaks of carrying in the body of the dying Jesus but expresses his boldness in speaking "because we know that the one who raised the Lord Jesus will raise us also with Jesus" (2 Cor 4:14). This reflection grows from a confession in which Paul celebrates the great gift of freedom: "The Lord is the Spirit; and where the Spirit of the Lord is, there is freedom" (3:17).

But can anyone live this self-abnegation alone? Are we not meant to live this daily dying of Jesus in a supporting community, with the hope of all meeting him in the resurrection? So it is not just that the Spirit teaches us to share gifts in community, but also to live, through the faith of the community, a deep sharing in the plan of God at work in history. A great work therefore of the Spirit is linking our mission to the memory of God's fidelity, ever-actualized in the celebration of Jesus' death and resurrection in the Eucharist. If the gift of the Spirit at Pentecost was understood as the inauguration of the final times, the gifts are for this "today" of the community, the living vibrant memory of promises made and promises fulfilled. Thus, Luke takes us back to the very beginnings and pushes us forward to the fullness of time (Acts

3:21), but only in and through the experience of taking up the cross daily, and together, in the power of the Spirit, of following Jesus. What a fabulous template over against which to measure the template of our life, four-score years if we are strong on this earth! (See Ps 90:10.) Coming to trust that one's life is caught up in the Spirit of God, working out the mystery of our salvation, is both the struggle and the delight of a lifetime in Christ.

Who has known the mind of God, who has been God's counselor? Living in the Spirit, the gift of Pentecost, we know spiritual things as only the Spirit gives us to know them. Yet there is a wisdom given us in Christ that no one has ever known, no one has yet divined. Truly all gifts need to be discerned in the community and tested at the bar of love. This wisdom sheds light on the gifts that we have received. It is always a revelation to discover that a community has the gifts that the present moment demands. The gift of Pentecost is ongoing, is always personal whether communitarian or individual, and always tailored to the demands and claims of the present situation. The energy released into the world by the gift of the Spirit is much more the gift of walking with the Risen Lord in the midst of life's daily demands and sufferings than it is any particular gift of tongues (glossolalia) or prophetic utterance. While always open to various gifts, the emphasis falls on the gift of love, not only our love for others, but God's love for us. This love accompanies us all the way to glory. Every other gift will pass away; even hope will yield to vision and faith to infused knowing, but love, the love of God for us, will remain forever. In this, many persons who pray the Rosary will discover the message of the spirituality of the heart of Jesus, for heart is the unique symbol, not of love, but of love discovered afresh! This love we discover each day is a love that looks at the world from the viewpoint of the one who is excluded. To pray this mystery of the Rosary may be to bring to the fore a gift that is both celebration and challenge.

†

Fourth Glorious Mystery

THE ASSUMPTION OF MARY

2 Kings 2:1–18, Psalm 16:9–10,
1 Corinthians 15:50,54–55

"Death has been swallowed up in victory."
(1 Cor 15:54)

"Death has been swallowed up in victory." These words of St. Paul, as we will read later, are crucial in the document issued by Pius XII in declaring Mary's assumption a dogma of the church.[9] Paul goes on to ask, "Where, O death, is your victory? / Where, O death, is your sting?" (1 Cor 15:55). The reason these words are appropriate for celebrating the assumption of Mary only becomes apparent gradually. Both *death as overcome in victory* and *assumption* are ways of speaking about the experience of the Risen Lord, insights gleaned through much contemplation. They belong to the end of Mary's life. There is an ancient axiom, in speaking of how God invades our human space, "the end time is like the first time." In fact, we often tell the beginning in light of where the story will end. Every time we tell the story of a person's life, we speak of the beginning and the end as extensions of the middle. This is a motif common in hagiography, the lives of the saints. We extol who the person was, not only in terms of their influence on others, but in terms of their life accomplishments reflected in the circumstances of their death back to their birth.

Both beginning and end are marked by divine favor. This is surely true of the story of Jesus. We find the same is true of Mary because she followed him. In the Preface for the feast of the ascension, we say of Jesus as Risen Lord: "Where you have gone, we hope to follow." As a disciple, Mary followed Jesus. Thus the contemplation of the ascension of Jesus has anticipated the assumption of Mary because where he went, she followed. Mary was *never* outside the need for Jesus. This long-held tradition of the faith community helped when Christians wanted to speak of the beginning of Mary's life. Tradition speaks of the immaculate conception; namely, that Mary, from the moment of her conception, was preserved from original sin. The hesitation of some to speak this way was relieved by the clarification that Mary was preserved only on the strength of the foreseen gracious outcome of the life, death, and resurrection of Jesus. The immaculate conception of Mary calls to mind the language of the Letter to the Romans 8:29–30 (see also Eph 1:5, 11):

> For those whom he foreknew he also predestined to be conformed to the image of his Son, in order that he might be the firstborn within a large family. And those whom he predestined he also called; and those whom he called he also justified; and those whom he justified he also glorified.

The word *predestined*, with its historical baggage, is problematic. It can be easily heard as a misconstruing of the relationship between God and a free human being. As cumbersome as the word sounds, *before-handedness* better expresses the initiative of

God with respect to Mary. The belief is that Mary's life was engulfed, from end to absolute beginning, by the presence to her of God in God's loving designs for all humankind. We will return to the preplanning on God's part in the contemplation of the Joyful Mystery of the Annunciation. Now, in the Mystery of the Assumption, we reflect on the symbol of God's engulfing the life of Mary at the end of her days on earth.[10]

There is no direct biblical text to which the community can point for Mary's assumption into heaven. The early community told a story about Mary's birth to Anna and Joachim. Also and more deliberately, following the liturgical refrain "where you have gone we hope to follow," the community told a story about her being taken from among us in a way reminiscent of the great ones in the story of salvation. There were many biblical analogies for the development of such a tradition. Jesus was taken up into heaven, and the disciples longingly looked up to heaven where he has gone (Acts 1:11). There are also the images of Enoch (Gen 5:24; Sir 49:49, 44:16; Heb 11:5) and of Elijah (2 Kgs 2:11; Sir 48:4–12), and in Judaism's Talmud and midrash, of Abraham and Moses. Mary takes her place among the great ones of Israel! Intertwined with the tradition of the assumption is the image of Mary's falling asleep (the "dormition of Mary"), an image beloved of the churches in the East.

Jesus died. As Risen Lord, he was assumed into heaven. Elijah, whose story is the most elaborate of the assumption stories in the scriptures, is taken up to heaven alive. The decree in 1950 published by Pius XII, declaring the assumption of Mary to be a matter of the church's long-cherished faith, speaks of the "dead body of the Blessed Virgin Mary." The degree concludes, having cited many witnesses from the ancient writers of the church,

Hence, the august Mother of God, mysteriously united for all eternity with Jesus Christ in one and the same decree of predestination, immaculate in her conception, a virgin inviolate in her divine motherhood, the whole-hearted companion of the divine Redeemer who won complete victory over sin and its consequences, gained at last the supreme crown of her privileges—to be preserved immune from the corruption of the tomb, and, like her Son, when death had been conquered, to be carried up body and soul to the exalted glory of heaven, there to sit in splendor at the right hand of her Son, the eternal King of the ages.[11]

One can see many reasons being offered for the assumption, some of which reflect the concerns of a church shaped by questions of bodiliness, virginity as opposed to marriage, and polarities of soul and body. In the same decree, there are hints of the more biblical concerns of victory over struggle and the ushering in of the final times in the unfolding of the history of salvation. For instance:

Above all it must be noted that from the second century the holy Fathers present the Virgin Mary as the new Eve, most closely associated with the new Adam, though subject to him in the struggle against the enemy from the nether world. This struggle, as the first promise of a redeemer implies, was to end in perfect victory over sin and death, always linked together in the writings of the apostle of the Gentiles. Therefore, just as the glorious resurrection of Christ was an essential part of this victory and its final trophy, so the struggle shared by the blessed Virgin and her Son was to end in the glorification of her virginal body.[12]

Pius XII then turns to the apostle Paul to conclude that paragraph: "As the same apostle says: 'when this mortal body has clothed itself in immortality, then will be fulfilled the word of Scripture: Death is swallowed up in victory.'"

The belief in the assumption of Mary goes beneath the biological facts of dying. There's a celebration of the life of one who has served God and for whom now God has come in a special way. Assumption is less a reward of the person's labors than a connection with those who remain. It is testimony to the passing of and the significance of one in whose life God worked out a special part of the divine plan of salvation.

We are used to a "last will and testament" from many biblical figures. The whole book of Deuteronomy is dedicated to Moses' last words. We hear the final words of Joshua in Joshua 24:1–28. Influenced by the previous two examples, an editor presents Solomon as closing his life with a wisdom speech (1 Kgs 8). Nothing prepares us for the prolonged last discourse of Jesus in John's Gospel, chapters 13–17, except perhaps the briefer but no less poignant farewell speech in Luke 22. Luke also gives us Paul's farewell speech at Miletus in Acts (20:17–38), and the disciples of Paul constructed his last testimony in 2 Timothy. We place the tradition of holy people being assumed at the end of their days within the wide scope of recording their last words, deeds, and gestures. These literary conventions function as a call to endurance on the journey. While the concern is to bring closure to people's lives in a time-honored way, the deeper concern is with the future. Were there nothing to hope for, there would be no need to hand on a testimony![13]

We return to a point raised earlier in this reflection. The issue is not *what* happened, but *why* did the community choose to present the story *this way*? What claim does the assumption of Mary make upon us? The temptation is to put Mary up on a pedestal and to think that all her titles and honors have nothing to do with my life. Wrong! What would the world be like were we to climb up and join her? Mary is no more than a faithful disciple. If her fidelity as a disciple elevates her, that's exactly the challenge of this mystery for us. Unless we envision such a bold response, the assumption of Mary, in the language of participation, falls to the ground. Our options are not to either deny Mary her pedestal or abandon her there. Instead, we are offered a simple invitation to take our place alongside her. Can we possibly believe that such may be true of us? After the initial shock of such a possibility, we know there is only one answer: Yes!

Is this not the "heavenly call of God in Christ Jesus" of which Paul speaks in Philippians 3:14? To live in glory! What was said earlier of Jesus is true of Mary. Just as Jesus did not shed his humanity in the gift of the resurrection, so too Mary did not shed her humanity in the time of God's transforming glory. The body I am now, in the midst of every relationship that I am, is the same body transformed into who I will be when I join the community of saints in glory. Every human relationship that was mediated through my body, often the source of pain and anguish in this earthly pilgrimage, will be transformed into life-giving and forgiving newness. The assumption of Mary prepares her to take her place in the march to glory spoken of by Paul (1 Cor 15:20–26). Join in with her. See all the people in traffic, shops, vacation resorts, parking lots, detention camps, and every job and profession walking with you. We are already counted in the multitudes without number in the Book of Revelation. Mary may be the woman clothed with the sun (Rev 12:1), but she would say that she was only being faithful to the grace given to her: "Greetings, favored one, the Lord is with you." The angelic salutation still rings clear with celebration, challenge, and assumption!

Over the course of praying many Rosaries and contemplating this mystery, there grows a profound conviction that *Yes,* God is actively faithful. Once God has loved us, God will never un-love us. We never become unclaimed baggage. God is never done with us. We experience the power to face the most down-to-earth tasks of our human journeying. We ask in retrospect: "How did we ever get through such and such?" As we face a new challenge, we ask, "What do we have to offer?" The image of the assumption as a participation in God's gift of endurance becomes for the Christian a way to interpret, in hope, so much of what is happening around us. New ground opens up for conversation and dialogue and deep listening through the fears and anxieties of our fellow travelers. If the ascension of Jesus has a strong missionary focus, the assumption of Mary is an assurance of accompaniment on the mission.

An intuition, born of the beads, of the divine involvement in our lot of being human nourishes our inner eye to enter even more deeply into the realities of modern life. Praying the Rosary engages us more deeply in the world that is explored in literature, music, arts, and the cinema. I have found that my love of the Rosary and my love of a good novel have a few points in common. Life's experiences get filtered through both. There is an at-homeness-in-the-world that develops in the person at prayer and in the same person in the midst of their literature and culture. The

Rosary, like the fine arts, relies on a rich inner world of meaning that is nourished through attention to feelings. And key to praying the Rosary is the contemplated human story unfolding in our lives this very day. There is nothing that cannot be woven into the kaleidoscope of the many mysteries that lead to the One Mystery. At the core of spiritual development there is a wealth of emotional intelligence, out of which emerges the process of evaluating the significance of even the most timeworn and ordinary experiences.

Some say that today's world is overstimulated. At any one time, there's too much to absorb. This is not an idle complaint. Focus, the fruit of living both from the inside-out and the outside-in, is therefore a must for integrated, centered living. In the great mysteries of our Christian religion, the believer can find focusing and centering images. The assumption of Mary makes a good candidate. Over against the experience of terror, anxiety, and ennui, we search for a purpose in the midst of randomness. Our modern culture may be wise enough not to look for a deus ex machina, an artificial or improbable force to resolve life's problems, but who doesn't dream of being "touched by an angel" when life's a cul-de-sac, a dead end? In the assumption of Mary, the Christian experiences again the truth that "love is strong as death, passion fierce as the grave" (Song 8:6).

However we may wish or not wish for a deus ex machina, we do not want to be treated as a machine ourselves. We want to be treated as persons, especially in the workplace. The assumption is a protest against using people and then discarding them. God not only claimed Mary to be in mission, but God claimed Mary forever. God never uses a person and then casts her or him away. Yes, a sword would pierce Mary's heart but her blessedness, God's blessedness in her, cannot ever be erased. Here the person praying the Rosary, who sees contemporary business using so many persons, shudders with gratitude at the sheer care of God for Mary. Catholic social teaching reminds us that in modern labor practices the person is never to be used and then cast aside without economic and social benefits. No matter how menial the task, a worker is always a person. The care shown for Mary in the assumption is the care God has for all who have borne the heat of the day. We are never without our inheritance, the ultimate symbol of participation. The belief here is not that the Assumption isn't an extraordinary gift of Mary, but rather a gift which we share with Mary through our incorporation into the inheritance of Christ through baptism. If stewardship is the management of one's inheritance, then assumption is the active involvement in that stewardship, the art of living with a deep regard for sustainability. Assumption opposes the fatalistic sabotage of human effort that is often promoted in an image of the final destruction of the world because the indelible dignity of being human will be sustained through many transformations. Luke seizes the profoundly human question—"Is that all there is?"—by responding with another question: "What must I do to inherit eternal life?" (10:25 and 18:18). Luke, the rhetorician, knowing well the transformative power of participation, says the answer is to love your neighbor and to embrace the poor. Mary, within the story of Jesus as hearer and doer of the word, assumed and active, appeals to the reader to become a member of this new missionary family, loving neighbor, both Gentile and Jew, and embracing the poor. Thus the assumption of Mary is a symbol for a pilgrim community that is welcoming and serves the poor.

I served as pastor for some years in a community known as Our Lady of the Assumption in New Bedford, Massachusetts.

The parish was founded in 1905 when the community struggled to find its own identity as immigrants from Cape Verde, not wanting to be known as "black Portuguese." Later, the community's original church building was damaged in a hurricane. In 1954, trying to acquire another piece of property, they had to purchase it through a white person because of racial prejudice. The explanation usually given for the name of the parish, Our Lady of the Assumption, is that their first property was acquired on August 15. However, given the active understanding of Mary assumed into glory presented above, can one not look back at these trials and struggles and see something of the deeper meaning of assumption: "What must I do to inherit eternal life?" Love your neighbor, never discard!

†

Fifth Glorious Mystery
MARY, QUEEN OF HEAVEN
Matthew 6:10, 1 Corinthians 15:20–28

"On earth as it is in heaven..."
(Matt 6:10)

Mary's total surrender to the overwhelming claim of God in the preaching of Jesus culminates in her coronation. In naming Mary queen, we recognize her response to God's claim upon the whole of her salient, socially conscious life for such is the energy in the icon of queen. In the Bible, there is no scene as such of the crowning of Mary; however, much in Sacred Scripture supplies the imagery of this mystery. The imagery of the woman with the crown of stars on her head (Rev 12) invites the Christian to interpret, out of the Book of Revelation, the title "Queen of Heaven." Students of apocalyptic literature recognize that an ending throws light on the beginning. This prompts the question: Does the Book of Genesis, the beginning of the Bible, offer a reflection on Revelation's queen and mother? How might the concerns of the author of Genesis aid our reflection on the theme of queenship?

Modern scholarship assigns the story about Adam and Eve in Genesis 2 and 3 to one author, or school of authors, called "Yahwist," writing in the ninth and eighth centuries BC. The biblical process of thinking through the bigger questions of God's promise to Israel by reflecting on contemporary scenes was already in use. The community was establishing an understanding of its contemporary experience of the kingship of David, whose reign began around 1000 BC, and its growing importance in the world. The experience of the covenant with God was now increasingly celebrated in Jerusalem. David developed a worship tradition that both praised God and upheld his political standing in the world. This connection with the temple gives plausibility to David as the origin of the psalms. The attribution to him would, of course, be magnified in long-distant hindsight. David's aspirations to build a temple materialized in the reign of Solomon. In many ways, the Yahwist writers were propagandists for the royal house, and the text's strength lies in its optimism and outreach. However, even from the first inklings of royalty in Israel's life, there were arguments against it. God is presented (see 1 Sam 8) as opposed to kingship for the very reasons that take David's life of grace to a life of disgraceful injustice. Nathan's reproof of David in 2 Samuel 12 echoes Samuel's detailed description of these reasons not to have a king.

Some scholars have argued that there are royal characteristics in the powers given to Adam and Eve, for better and for worse. Could the illicit relationship of David with Bathsheba have been the model that the author used in depicting Adam and Eve? The Bible never hides David's sin. Does it also use the sin of David to depict original sin? In the Genesis stories, there is no hint that the sin was sexual. Nathan's rebuke of David was not that his sin was a breach of sexual mores but a breach of boundaries, the misuse of his royal authority to deprive Uriah of his wife, Bathsheba. Is the author challenging, in his depiction of Adam, the hubris of the reign of David, the man who failed to live within boundaries and respect limits? Eve is presented as testing boundaries in the scene with the serpent when she exaggerates the demands of God, telling the serpent that "God said, 'You shall not eat of the fruit of the tree that is in the middle of the garden, nor shall you touch it, or you will die,'" whereas God's prohibition referred only to eating (Gen 3:3, contrasted with 2:17). In David, the author who gives us Adam and Eve had an example of refusing boundaries. David broke bounds and transgressed.

The author took the story of David to sort out the issues at stake in the beginning of the story of salvation. But was the author influenced by the part played by Bathsheba? One may not expect a major development of queenship in such a patriarchal tradition. However, mention of who was queen was not put aside. In fact, the royal tradition never overlooked the place of Bathsheba in the family of David (2 Sam 11). She was the queen mother of Solomon, in whom the covenant made with the throne of David was passed on. Also, her influence was sought when Adonijah, another son of

David's, conspired to take the king's place on the throne. No less than Nathan, the same prophet who censured David for taking Bathsheba from Uriah, said to her: "Now therefore come, let me give you advice, so that you may save your own life and the life of your son Solomon" (1 Kgs 1:5, 11-12).

How did the story of David and Bathsheba influence the story of Genesis? Chapters 1–11 in Genesis, the overture to the entire Bible, are an introduction to the cycle of Abraham stories, chapters 12–23. The author is giving the reason why God called Abraham. Humankind has sinned and is in need of salvation. In Abraham, all the peoples of the earth will find blessing. God made a promise to the patriarch, and then, in virtue of that promise, called to himself a people, Abraham's descendents, out of Egypt, and gave those people a land. The irony is that the very person, David, with whose throne God unilaterally made a covenant, is the one whose story epitomizes the need for salvation. The Yahwist author may be David's court theologian, but he is not shy to point to the reality of sin. Hence, to name the need for a story of salvation, he does not look further than the behavior of the very king of Israel. The suggestion is that the sin of David fuels the Genesis description of the fall of Adam and Eve. David is not the one being extolled. God is being praised because God, despite David's abuse of his royal power, is faithful to the covenant made with him.

But what does this have to do with Mary the Queen of Heaven? I suggest that in giving Mary the royal title Queen of Heaven, the Christian community brings into the contemplation of the mystery of Christ, unfolding in Mary, all that was captured in the royal imagery of the Bible. That imagery carries both grace and disgrace, including the abuse of royal power in the exploitation of women, an example of which we see in the David-Bathsheba story. If the story of Eve was built on the David-Bathsheba story, the image of Mary as the new Eve, presented, for instance, in the papal decree proclaiming the assumption, reverses that story. This reversal of what we have come to expect from political institutions and structures not only relates to the spirituality of Mary but also, more radically, to the transformative way that God lays claim to the world in the ministry of Jesus Christ.

The greatest development of the Rosary was in a time when, through the lives of many kings and queens, the monarchical structure experienced Christian transformation.[14] Many of the royalty of this period were canonized: King Wenceslaus of Bohemia (907–35), Queen Elizabeth of Hungary (1207–31), and King Louis of France (1214–70). People found in them a great unification of faith and social justice. Some of the biblical values in the hoped-for Messiah (for example, Isaiah 9 and 11), realized in Jesus, were seen as exemplified in the lives of these saints. The expectations of the ordinary people were reversed when these saints merged well the templates of biblical imagery and lived experience. Since the days of Pius XI, it is true that Catholic social teaching has highly valued democracy as a form of political and social organization; however, the teaching does not espouse any political form as the sole political structure capable of interpreting God's claim upon humankind. The challenge for the modern Christian is to know that imagery of the Bible, its energy, and its scope, and to find what is analogous in our modern experience of political structures. There is no way to live in this world without language and social structure. Both language and structure ever evolve and are in need of constant adaptation and renewal. Borrowing the language of the human institution of royalty, to call Mary Queen of Heaven is a summons to such an adaptation, transformation, and renewal. There is nothing of our story today that cannot be surrendered to grace!

We began our reflection on this mystery with the statement that Mary's coronation symbolizes her final surrender to the overwhelming claim of God in Christ. In imaging God-in-Christ undoing the fall of Adam and Eve, which was perhaps modeled by the Yahwist on the seduction of Bathsheba by David, Mary as the new Eve, the mother of all the living (Gen 3:20), represents hope for restored dignity and self-respect. Mary's free gift of participation in the story of God's love, which would resist exploitation or harassment even by a king, transforms what it means to be crowned a queen. Is it not from a search for such dignity and sense of belonging that we come to honor Mary? Does such an image give a person the courage never to settle for less than their God-given dignity and belonging?

Honoring Mary as Queen of Heaven places her paradoxically with the pilgrim community on earth. The feast of the queenship of Mary is celebrated on the octave of the assumption. Her coronation explores what we mean by "heaven" when we pray the words of Jesus in the Our Father: "Your will be done on earth as in heaven." But the significance of the coronation is not just for life in heaven but also for life on earth. Coronation then is total surrender to total claim not just at the end of life on earth but while we are a pilgrim people. The "as on earth" template shuns any flight from the world. It's a defense against the accusation of otherworldliness leveled at certain Christians. As *Jesus Christ Superstar*, the hit musical of the 1970s put it, these Christians have "too much heaven on their minds" to be involved in the everyday problems "on earth."[15] Instead of a means to escape life in this world, the hope of glory expressed in both the assumption and coronation of Mary engages us even more completely in the structures of this world.

Where do we begin? As elemental as it may sound, we live "on earth as it is in heaven" only in and through the body. There is no human who has not been born from another's body. We are each other's body, and there's no other way to participate in life. As body, we are made for relationship, and the transformation of the body is the transformation of all the relationships we have, the relationships we are. Paul, for one, notes that the person as body is made for resurrection and glory (1 Cor 6:13). And in the same letter, he shares this momentous understanding of belonging in the community: "All belong to you, and you belong to Christ and Christ belongs to God" (3:22–23). So the person called in the body to glory is the person in all his and her relationships. Paul's discussion of the human body in its many transformations underscores the search for identity and belonging, a major concern of modern life. Catholic social teaching holds that the human person, as God's image and likeness, carries this hope of glorious transformation into all creation. Despite myriad situations of sin and disgrace, humans never lose that dignity in their search for belonging. The visualization of the goal of our lives in Mary's crowning as the new Eve, Queen of Heaven, gives us the endurance to join the search.

In light of recalling the need to live here on earth as an embodied people, the communion of saints takes on a whole new dynamism. One can view the feasts of the communion of saints, All Saints' Day and All Souls' Day, as the Christian understanding of the praise of ancestors. Praise of our ancestors recollects our literal origins, and the communion of saints looks to where we are going. In our many cultural expressions, we enshrine those from whom we received life, be it a visit to a Shinto shrine or carrying a photo lovingly in one's wallet. We know who we are when we name our ancestors and know our roots. Dignity follows belonging. We know who we are when we recognize to whom we belong.

Mary's coronation, surrender to total claim, is never to be isolated from the communion of saints. This simple image of going to glory together, in the communion of those to whom we belong in Christ, questions much of the individualism that too often characterizes church teaching about the end of life. How easy it is for us to misinterpret the final scene: the individual person appearing alone before the judgment seat of God, in the absence of Christ. The separation of the particular judgment and the general judgment has undermined many good persons as they approach death. Lost is the belief that we come before God in Christ. "In Christ" means in a communion of saints. The more emphasis we place on these key insights, the more life-giving is the image of Mary, our sister disciple, one of the communion of those whose robes have been washed in the Blood of the Lamb (Rev 7:14). This allusion to the Book of Revelation locates the prayer of the person saying the Rosary within the praise and worship of God, whose claim upon us in Christ, in the face of chaos, holds the community together.

This mystery of Mary Queen of Heaven is associated in the church's prayers (August 22) with Mary Queen of Peace. This resonance between titles leads us to explore the pursuit of peace as a duty of royalty. No throne is ever held onto without constant struggle against chaos, the enemy of peace. Waging war was the prerogative or duty of, but also at times a tactic abused by, kings. The prophets pointed out such abuse and initiated a long confrontation with the ideologies of war and the addiction to militarism. They urge us to pursue peace in a way that increasingly refuses violence. God's victory will be won on God's terms. Peace is always the fruit of victory in the struggle for dignity and belonging. Peace is the fruit of God's victory of grace, as the crowning of God's creatures in heaven symbolizes in this mystery of the Rosary. This victory of grace is achieved through the transformation of many political structures and their corresponding ideologies. Peace, shalom, the gift of a God covenanted with God's people, became the symbol of the gift of God's kingdom. Jesus is the prince of peace. His disciples are to announce the arrival of God's claim by announcing peace. "Peace to this house!" is a proclamation that cannot be rejected with impunity (Luke 10:5). Peace is the gift of the missionary Risen Lord as presented in John's Gospel, coupled with an empowerment to forgive sin (20:19–23). Mary is queen because she is claimed by the paschal greeting of peace, sure sign of the presence of the kingdom.

A devotion to Mary Queen of Peace, which I view as set within the veneration that responds to the crowning of Mary in heaven, is a way "to live on earth as in heaven." This devotion celebrates God's action in Mary's life, in and through Jesus through the power of the Holy Spirit. And in the thinking of Pius XII, the celebration is of victory in the struggle for justice that marks our human journey. These carefully made distinctions are not without purpose to understand well a devotion to Mary Queen of Peace. Peace is a summons to surrender to the claim of God over this earth that the crowning of Mary in heaven symbolizes. In an inspired rereading of Isaiah 52:7, Luke in Acts 10:36 presents God as announcing peace in Jesus: "You know the message which he sent to the people of Israel, preaching peace by Jesus Christ." Isaiah 52:7, the text from which we get the word *gospel,* carries the note of announcing victory. "How beautiful upon the mountains / are the feet of the messenger / who announces peace, / who brings good news, / who announces salvation, / who says to Zion, 'Your God reigns.'" Ultimately, every struggle is a struggle for social justice. The struggle is social, legal, spiritual, and cosmic. Psalm 72—what we could call the job description of the king—presents the promotion of social justice as the unique role of monarchy. If we commit to this struggle for social justice, the lasting and only worthy obligation of a king, we will be surprised by the gift of peace! To use the phrase attributed to Paul VI, if you want peace, work for justice. The king's greatest victory is not the vanquishing of external enemies but the procurement of peace built on justice at home. When such conditions do not prevail at home, then the land is ripe to be taken over by outsiders who promise more but, in fact, deliver less. The prophets, who were the watchdogs of the king's fulfillment of his job description, inveigh more against internal corruption than against external enemies. What people today do not suffer the effects of political corruption? These insights remind us that, within Luke' plot, we are always moving toward the city of peace, Jerusalem. This is the city that needs to recognize its hour of visitation and what makes for peace (19:42) and, for the Rosary contemplative, a symbol of every human structure that needs adaptation and transformation. To say that God announces peace and that peace is God's gift is not to promote a return to Quietism, a seventeenth-century movement of disengagement, but, rather, to actively promote the victory of the peacemaker.

Mary's Magnificat echoes all the demands made of the king to promote justice. Her crowning therefore is no empty gesture. It vindicates her revolutionary spirituality, one with that of the *anawim*, the poor that struggled and cried out for justice. To all who struggle for respect and human dignity within the structures of our lives, this devotion to Mary as Queen of Peace, the new Eve, vindicated and crowned as Queen of Heaven, would come as a great consolation. There will be no gift of peace until we stand in a communion of saints-to-be, together on this earth, and refuse any attempt to exploit and efface our God-given human dignity and respect.

At the end of a day, it is customary in many religious communities to sing the Salve Regina (Hail, Holy Queen) after Compline (Night Prayer). In my own religious community, many times the brothers or sisters sing the song facing a statue of Our Lady Queen of Peace. When we sing of the valley of tears through which we are passing, my longing is for joy, the effusion of peace. As we now move on to the Joyful Mysteries, we are already—thanks to the glorious mysteries of the resurrection, ascension, gift of the Holy Spirit, assumption, and coronation—united with those who gave us the stories on which these mysteries of joy are built.

4

THE JOYFUL MYSTERIES

†

First Joyful Mystery
THE ANNUNCIATION TO MARY
Luke 1:26–38

"Greetings, favored one! The Lord is with you."
Luke 1:28

Each time we pray the Rosary, there is a new adventure, even in territory already familiar to us. The Joyful Mysteries, with the birth of Jesus at their center, never lose their ability to surprise for being familiar. This is not unlike our own birth stories, still waiting, for all their familiarity, to be fully unfolded.

Stories of beginnings and endings, these are the stuff of life, and how often have we told a story in terms of its outcome. A story is told again and again, dressed up to meet the challenges of the time in which it is told. An engaging quality of all good art and literature is always what can also be read into and out of a storyline.

The people who gave us the Bible enjoyed this kind of story-telling. There are stories to explain why people are named as they are, and stories to explain why they live the way they do. This is called *the etiological motif* in stories and is but one of the many ways in which a living vibrant tradition expresses itself. What drives the storytelling is an experience in the present in which the story is being relived, is still relevant, and still energizes the hearers. Bible stories answer the question why, not out of idle curiosity, but out of a very profound conviction that the story ultimately leads us to an ever-faithful and caring God. The story leaves its original moorings and appears in some other place, or in some other situation in life, attached or not attached to the immediate story of Israel's odyssey with God or to the early community's memory of Jesus. It is the art of biblical study to trace these social and narrative seams and to suggest from where the story may have come and how it developed along the way.

Few places in scripture are more interesting in such a pursuit than the infancy narratives about Jesus from which collection we draw the five Joyful Mysteries.[1] The reading of holy books is part of every great religion and is the more fruitful to the extent that it asks us to focus on our own experience of telling stories and building a tradition. I hope we never read the infancy narrative of Matthew and Luke without thinking of the story of our own birth. Here is a template for us already at hand. With life's experience and the birth, perhaps, of our own children, the story will grow, becoming a story within a story. Of course, stories both enhance and heal. Just as relationships laid down alongside relationships can bring healing and hope, fresh joy and new love, so too stories, which always deal with relationships, bring newness and life. For many children, hearing a bedtime story brings a day to a close because parents know that a good story can bring rest and peace to a young heart.

The story of the birth of Jesus came early to the growing community. True, Mark didn't give us one and John recast the story in another direction that broadens the perspective, "the Word became flesh" (1:14). Matthew and Luke received a developing but fragmentary tradition from their communities, already quite distinct from one another. In fact, each evangelist's story was only adequately understood in each evangelist's own setting and religious perspective. They have many aspects in common but the differences are very telling. For Matthew, the annunciation is to Joseph although there is a clear indication of an unexpected pregnancy. For Luke, the annunciation is to Mary and the pregnancy is of a virginal conception. Matthew seemed to be in a hurry to move beyond the birth, the story of which is like a big footnote (1:18–25), explaining the difficulties in the final phase of the genealogy of Jesus. He then concentrated on the stories when Jesus was a young child (2:1–23). Luke was not without his share of childhood stories, but he concentrated more than Matthew on the details of the birth and on what immediately preceded and followed the event (1:5—2:52).

Luke cast the annunciation to Mary as the call of a prophetess. This reminds us of all the calls ever made to persons to be part of the long story of God's courting Israel. Call-stories are telling exposés of the humanness of the people with whom God wants to work. God seldom receives an immediate answer; there are issues to be discussed and even, at times, confirmatory signs to be sought. Some decline for want of skill, others for want of a family tradition, and others for want of age and experience; God disregards all these excuses and keeps calling. As this form of introduction was used, it allowed the person's disciples, acting as editors even of oral traditions, to showcase his or her major message, tell why the message endured, and indeed explain why the person was counted among that very special group of people, "the prophets."

The prophet's role made him or her bigger than life, and the faith of the community itself was communicated in the telling of the prophet's "career." Isaiah, Jeremiah, and Ezekiel—each one's very personal life becomes identified with the message, and vice versa. The demands made on each are great and at times, more than one can bear. Ezekiel's quixotic behavior still challenges our ordinary expectations. He didn't even mourn the death of his wife, she who was "the delight of [his] eyes" (Ezek 24:15–17). We have in the story of Isaiah of Jerusalem the whole history of Israel, personalized in that the prophet was utterly claimed by the purpose of God in history, the mystery of God's saving plan revealed only to the prophets. Isaiah gives us the songs of the Suffering Servant of Yahweh (Isa 42:1–7, 49:1–7, 50:4–9, 52:53—53:12) in which we can no longer distinguish between the life of the prophet and the life of the community.

As we noted earlier, kings in Israel were reluctantly accepted. Prophets were called to keep the kings honest in their service to the claims of God over peoples, nations, the earth, the universe. In doing their job, the prophets themselves became totally absorbed by the claim of God. Ezekiel eats a scroll! (Ezek 3:1–3; see also Rev 10:9-10). This is bizarre but only to one who doesn't know the depth of this claim upon our lives! Jeremiah says in his confessions: "If I say, 'I will not mention him, / or speak any more in his name,' / then within me there is something like a burning fire / shut up in my bones; / I am weary with holding it in, and I cannot" (20:9). Earlier, Jeremiah cries, "O Lord, you have enticed me, and I was enticed" (20:7), but he would not have God's claim any other way.

Mary knows. Mary's yielding to the claim of God upon her sets the theme for the entire presentation of Luke's Gospel. Luke presents Jesus as prophet, and the community as the community of the missionary and prophetic word to the entire world (Luke 4:16–30, especially 22). But only after contemplating Luke's presentation of Jesus as prophet does the reader return to appreciate all the more with what sharply prophetic strokes Luke depicted Mary. She is clearly in the prophetic tradition as one whose life has been irresistibly claimed by a God who is faithful to every word spoken. It's no wonder that Luke uses the convention of a prophetic call-story in presenting the annunciation.

But there is more! In the annunciation scene, the faith of Israel and the faith of the Christian community are marvelously interwoven and expressed. The creed of the early community about its heritage in the spirituality of Israel and Judaism is stitched into the early steps of this annunciation story. The angel says, "He will be great, and will be called the Son of the Most High, and the Lord God will give to him the throne of his ancestor David. He will reign over the house of Jacob forever and of his kingdom there will be no end" (1:32–33). Mary has a typically prophetic objection: "How can this be since I am a virgin?" Gabriel says, "The Holy Spirit will come upon you, and the power of the Most High will overshadow you; therefore the child to be born will be holy; he will be called Son of God" (v. 35). God will fulfill the promise made to the throne of David. In Mary, God is being faithful to that claim. While that claim of God, honored in the extraordinary events of her birthing of Jesus, puts Mary in the big picture, the contemplative question is, Does Mary's calling give a bigger framework to all childbearing? What has Mary to say to parents? Can God make a greater claim on anyone than to bring a child into this world?

Perhaps no claim upon us is more open to a myriad of feelings and interpretations than the news of pregnancy. With natural family planning, the news that one's going to be a parent, and especially a mother, may not be surprising. It is, nonetheless, filled with a sense of adventure. People throughout the world have many reasons to bear a child: to form a family, to give our parents a grandchild, to assure that our name lives on, to maintain the family farm or business, to help liberate one's people from an occupying force, to propagate a religion.

In some parts of our world today, the fear of bringing a girl to birth is terrifying. In China, where boys are preferred and only one child is permitted per couple, parents often hide the news of the birth of a girl. From countries having such a restrictive policy, there are many stories of fathers and mothers anguishing over their children. In some parts of India, girls are unwanted because the dowry that will be asked of them at the time of their marriage is too much. Many girls are put to death, often poisoned and the body burned. The person joyfully contemplating Mary's pregnancy is stopped short on hearing these painful reports. Because these practices are an affront to the human dignity modeled by Mary, the Christian is invited into the tension and struggle of contemporary life. The sadness of a birth denied, however, does not falsify what the Christian believes about the will of God for the dignity of human beings, but in fact makes living "on earth as in heaven" all the more relevant.

In contemplating this mystery, every birth becomes an event of extraordinary compass, never again a mere statistic. Today it is clearly recognized that the problem of overpopulation is the result of poor politics and the uneven distribution of the world's wealth. For the contemplative, outraged both by the inequity of wealth and by the use of infanticide to solve personal or national problems, there emerges a commitment to the education of women worldwide. Education is the only antidote to the systematic exclusion of women from making choices, in dialogue with the traditions of human dignity and belonging, about their own bodies.[2]

The ideology shaping these painful experiences of infanticide is that the norm for being human is male. That is the most pernicious ideology that rakes the world today and underpins not only patriarchy but also massive poverty. The church itself must seriously question its own ideologies and leave them open to the critique of the gospel. Mary's annunciation sets the stage for Luke's presentation that questions all our assumptions and our too facilely justified dogmatic statements. The template of the world we live in and the template of Mary clash around the origin of our joy: Is our joy the fruit of controlling our world through the dominance of the powerful or the fruit of a community of awareness working together for the inclusion of all? Mary's blessedness was that she could live joyfully with the divine upending of every human expectation. The good news will be a world built from the margins and from the subversion of those holding a controlling power in the center. In the annunciation, the gospel who is Jesus is already making its claim on this new world. Parents need to be assured that bringing a child into this world is a great honor and privilege to be welcomed and supported. Such a vision, nurtured and developed by the one contemplatively praying the Rosary, lends itself effectively to the attitudes and mind-set necessary for the realization of the so-called Millennium Development Goals, a program initiated by the United Nations for the eradication of half of world poverty by 2015, and embraced by John Paul II in his

message on peace, January 2005. Today, every birth calls for inten-
sive care. The maternity ward and emergency room converge.

Mary, claimed for childbearing, is totally committed. Her
youthfulness and depth of spirituality, the clarity of her questioning, and the spontaneity of her response are all involved. This
involvement is an enormously exciting and joyful claim made
upon persons praying this mystery. Do we dare say with her, as
in Luke 1:38: "Here I am, the servant of the Lord; let it be with me
according to your word"? Our Christian faith invites us, like
Mary, to answer in the affirmative because Mary trusted what
Paul would discover later, the promise in God's words: "My
grace is sufficient" (2 Cor 12:9).

How did Mary know that God's grace would be sufficient?
Perhaps the word *sufficient* leaves us cold and sounds calculating.
But behind the word there is an exuberance, and it is all part of the
angel's greeting: "Greetings, favored one! The Lord is with you"
(1:28). There is no understanding Mary without exploring this pregnant greeting. Mary's blessedness is the action of God. In speaking
earlier of the titles of Mary, I mentioned the grace that preceded
Mary's life. The student of the Bible is challenged to adequately
translate what the original Greek conveys. Let me show you why.
Grammatically, the greeting is put in the pluperfect, or present
perfect, passive participle; for example, "You have been favored."
The passive voice indicates divine action, the pluperfect participle
means some action once done but now still powerfully effective.
The Greek verb actually means "graced," from which we draw the
meaning of being gifted. And all of this is in the vocative case, a
direct address to Mary, a greeting with all the sense of surprise and
even shock and, furthermore, trembling. So, in essence, the angel

says, "Greetings to you claimed irresistibly by gift of God, from long before now and be assured that I walk with you forever!"

After that assurance, is there anyone who wants to go to Bethlehem with Mary, the mother-to-be?

†

Second Joyful Mystery

MARY'S VISIT WITH ELIZABETH

Luke 1:39–56

"The child in my womb leaped for joy."
(Luke 1:44)

In his Prologue, Luke describes his Gospel as "an orderly account of the events that have been fulfilled among us" (1:1–4). And so he tells the story in order, although looking at all events retrospectively in light of the resurrection of Jesus. Thus Luke gives the reader, perhaps a Gentile-become-Christian, the context in which to interpret not only these wonderful events of birth but all that will follow. To begin, Luke opens with not one but two annunciation stories. The visitation, coming after the two annunciations but before the two births, acts as a bridge and sets the tone for the proper interpretation of what is happening.

The first annunciation scene is set in the temple, where Zechariah was serving as priest and offering incense in the sanctuary. He and his wife, Elizabeth, are extolled as righteous and as observant of the Torah, and yet they are childless. Gabriel's appearance in the sanctuary is presented as a prophetic call-story.

Zechariah, like Mary, raises objections, in his case to the possibility of a son in his advanced age. The sign given him is his own speechlessness until the child to be born is named John. After the boy's naming, Zechariah's speechlessness gives way to praise, and in his canticle (1:67–79), he expands on the place of John, his son, in the story of salvation. Zechariah develops themes first broached in the angel's greeting to him (1:10–20). Already it is clear that God's claim upon us of good news is in reversal of all human expectation, a theme which Mary's own canticle marvelously describes (1:46–55).

Mary's annunciation we have already discussed in the First Joyful Mystery. Before she gives her "Yes" to God, the angel Gabriel tells her that her elderly kinswoman Elizabeth is pregnant, for nothing is impossible with God. Soon after, Mary travels to the hill country to be with her cousin. At Mary's greeting, Elizabeth feels within her body, for the first time, the fulfillment of the angel's words to Zechariah. She and Zechariah know they will have the joy and gladness of a son and that many will rejoice at his birth (1:15). Thus the joy of the visitation (1:44) echoes the joy of the annunciation of the birth of John the Baptist (1:14), which had swiftly drawn up, in one image, the hope of Israel: "He will turn many of the people of Israel to the Lord their God" (v. 16). With John's birth, Luke anticipates the messianic joy of the fulfillment of God's promises that marks the ultimate claim of the kingdom upon us.

After Mary's first greeting, Elizabeth says, "Blessed are you among women....And blessed is she who believed that there would be a fulfillment of what was spoken to her by the Lord" (1:42, 45). Both Elizabeth's experience of joy and her beatitude addressed to Mary discern the elements of Mary's vocation: trust joy! Elizabeth invites every generation of readers into a new place in terms of having confidence in God's ways of being faithful.

In the face of such joyful trust in God's fidelity, can anyone be mistrustful of their own calling? The template for the person praying the Rosary is the question, Where in my life do I have the assurance that God will walk with me? In contemplation of the various call-stories within the Bible, I discern this assurance: As we are made in God's image, hearers of God's word, there is no one *un*-called in all of creation. We discern our calling in the midst of our human becoming and development. Yes, each person is different and our personal make-up determines how we may feel and express joy. Always, even under the burden of resolving many doubts, we need to ask: Do we have joy, trembling, sheer exuberance, and even passion as confirmation? In each personal discernment there is an assurance felt, like a child moving in the womb, that were I to take this step, God would walk with me "and guide our feet into the way of peace" (Luke 1:79).

We speak of the Christian calling in reference to many different ways of living one's life through faith in Jesus Christ. With the recognition that all are called to holiness in all that we do, the importance of discerning one's personal life choices emerges more strongly. Christian vocation refers to following Jesus, not primarily whether we are married or single, lay or religious. The decision to follow Jesus as married people demands in-depth discernment. Since Vatican II, the elements of personal bonding and friendship, alongside the procreative purpose of marriage, are increasingly seen as important and the grounds for much discernment. We are accustomed by now in the practice of pre-Cana programs to discerning not only the gifts to be married but the combination of skills and gifts needed to be married to this or that particular person.

To give birth is another discernment! For the Christian, to raise a child is a singularly privileged sharing in the task of evangelization, a vocation shared by father and mother. Christians share with the Jewish and Muslim parent the desire to pass on to their offspring the gifts of their own faith. With today's complexities, the challenge of parenthood is a commitment to prepare the child to live his or her faith within deep layers of diversity and cultural pluralism. What a joy to discern the calling of one's children within one's own calling to educate them to use their skills for the betterment of the world.

Elizabeth and Zechariah are called to prepare their son to take his place in the unfolding of the human family. They would have trembled, yet also smiled, to have so envisioned the vocation of their son within their own vocation to give him birth. Zechariah's canticle, in which he expands on the angel's description of John's vocation, can be understood in terms of responsible stewardship. Our commitment to manage well the heritage that we have received is our duty, renewing the spirit and power of Elijah "to turn the hearts of parents to their children" (see Mal 4:6, also Sir 48:10). John's task is to build a just world in solidarity with the oppressed and the marginalized as was noted earlier in our reflection on the baptism of Jesus. This is pre-evangelization and all the world religions need to have dialogue on a mission similar to that of John the Baptist, preparing the human family to live in solidarity. Treating every human being with dignity is a goal that all of us can share, and the common ground for any assessment of what we do. Modern world events, not least the devastating earthquakes and tsunami in the South Indian Sea and the triple hurricanes in the Gulf Coast, have pressed upon us the need to clarify the betterment of humankind as the primary goal of religion, in which the support of any other vocation, however religiously interpreted, should stand. The deepest meaning of every human life is to make a contribution to a "human ecology." This expression, taken from John Paul II's discussion of solidarity in his 1991 encyclical *Centenimus Annus,* and which is worthy of Zechariah's canticle, pushes us then to see our calling first in terms of the world and the quality of life for all.

I suggest that Elizabeth and Zechariah's calling to prepare John's calling, a vocation within a vocation, parallels the calling today of parents to nurture the calling of their children for the generations ahead. Is this not the promise that all will find blessing in Abraham (Gen 12:3)? Zechariah blesses God who "has shown the mercy to our fathers promised to our ancestors, / and has remembered his holy covenant, / the oath that he swore to our ancestor Abraham, / to grant us that we, being rescued from the hands of our enemies, / might serve him without fear in holiness and righteousness / before him all our days" (Luke 1:72–75).

Within this wider calling to stewardship, Mary's discernment with Elizabeth invites comment on the discernment of gifts to serve in the Christian community. Luke was aware of the interpersonal conflicts between Christians because he was writing for communities where Paul, his erstwhile missionary companion, had experienced much difficulty. Let Paul's relationship with the communities of Corinth be a clear indication, not only of the excitement of finding that you are now somebody in the community, but of the stress in discerning what gifts, in the sense of what skills, are important for the building up of the community. Imagine a young man or woman, coming from the surrounding mountain areas and finding work in Corinth. In a search for belonging and identity, he or she starts going with friends to this newly found Christian community. Suddenly, the newly arrived finds him- or herself capable of fitting in, with skills and talents needed for the mission, and with an accepting community wherein to celebrate them. Would not such a person be in need of discerning these gifts and knowing how to work along with others' gifts, their likes and dislikes?

In answering the need of these new Christians, Paul discusses the variety of gifts. He establishes love as the highest. Love is the test that any one gift at any given time is from the Spirit. This gift of love is not only the love with which one brother or sister receives another member of the community, no matter their social status, but the love with which God loves all of us. This discernment undercuts any pride, arrogance, envy of another's gifts, or jealousy of one's own gifts that can hurt a community. Let each brother or sister identify with gratitude his or her gifts. This is much more important than comparing or contrasting one's gifts with those of another. Members are called to rejoice in each other's gifts. All are important. All stand on the strength of the gift of God's love, God's claim upon us in this community at this time.[3]

Luke Gospel's suggests a special way to know whether a Christian has moved beyond comparisons and contrasts, owned his or her own gifts, and stood solidly on the experience of God's gift of love. Is there joy? Is there the evident release of joy? The lasting insight Elizabeth and Mary give to us to understand their discerning interaction is the release of joy. This is their way of discerning gifts for the service of the community. In the exchange, Elizabeth is vocal, joyfully praising God and upholding her younger kinswoman. Both their gifts are integral to the unfolding of God's plan of salvation. Elizabeth's considerably significant gift of "fertile sterility" is immense. Taking words from the ancient rabbis, "how much the more" is Mary's gift of virginal conception. But the truly insightful issue is not the comparison of gift with gift but the celebration of the freedom of God's planning and gifting the community at this time. It is simply grace to be able to see the bigger picture, and this is why these two women could so deeply rejoice in each other's gifts. Can joy be so important to us in building community?

This template, celebrating gifts in service to community, cannot be lost on the person today finding his or her way in the local Christian community. The situation is not unlike that of Corinth—in fact, there's very much the same search for belonging and identity. Similarly, many Catholic communities today are thirsting for persons gifted with skills—interpersonal, pastoral, organizational, and visionary—for ministry.

The Catholic church stands today at a crossroads, having gone for so long on a model of clerical ministry and now finding that single model is no longer adequate. The church has awakened in some places and is searching to respond to the present crisis. While there is much to do to attract well-educated lay persons to positions of ministry, a parallel need is the process of transformation that comes from reflection on the lived experience of gift given and lived for others. The instrument for ministry is one's own person in the constant process of being transformed. That transformation comes from prayerful reflection on the joyful experience of God working for the good of others in and through one's own gifts and skills.[4]

Elizabeth and Mary modeled a process now much cherished as the central plank on which Christian community builds: an inductive reflection on experience; that is, they put words on their experience of God. The great community builder in the early Christian movement, Paul the apostle to the Gentiles, illustrates the lesson that the two women give us. For instance, when Paul comes to cry out that the call and gift of God are irrevocable (Rom 11:29), he has reached an enormously rich grasp of the Christian gospel on the relationship of Jew and Gentile in the divine plan of salvation. That way forward is worked out in Luke through reflection on experience, as in the story of Peter and Cornelius (Acts 11:19–26). Thus the Christian communities that had struggled with the question for a long time came to grasp a foundational missionary insight: the freedom of the Giver of the Gifts! Paul learned in Corinth what I am calling the visitation model of discernment (that all is gift, 1 Cor 4:7), which he applied in Rome (the gifts and call are irrevocable, Rom 11:29). The test is joy, evidence of the presence of the Spirit. When the community in Antioch received the decisions of the Council in Jerusalem on these weighty missionary questions, they rejoiced. "So they [the messengers] were sent off [from Jerusalem] and went down to Antioch. When they gathered the congregation together, they delivered the letter. When its members read it, they rejoiced at the exhortation" (Acts 15:30–31; the letter referred to is described earlier in vv. 22–29). This is most appealing to one who prays the Rosary because, in contemplation, we are doing the very same thing: reflecting on experience as a way to trust joy.

One parenting lesson of the Mystery of the Visitation is that our stumbling and faltering to live in giftedness have been foreseen and already embraced by a God who never takes back the call given and the gift received. Jesus embraced, as part of the necessity laid upon him, the reality that we would not know the hour of our visitation (Luke 19:44). But in love, the greatest of all the gifts, God will wait us out and be present to us when we finally get it. How often have parents suffered watching their children flounder until they discover their giftedness and then move on in life! From her visit with her kinswoman, Mary knew that being a mother would mean walking with Jesus and turning many things over and over in her heart as he grew and developed and named his giftedness before God and his fellow human beings. I suggest that Luke would have rejoiced to no end in the scene in John's Gospel in which Jesus on the cross says to the disciple whom he loved, "Here is your mother" (19:25–27). Luke knew that the church would have to hear "here is your mother" over and over again to know how to live in giftedness, to walk in the handmaid's lowliness, and to rejoice that, as Mary trusted, "all generations will call me blessed" (Luke 1:48).

How about imagining a baby shower as the template for the Mystery of the Visitation, for which Gabriel already named the gifts? Elizabeth as kinswoman, full of the spirit, brought joy! Mary was not embarrassed to have brought the same: the joy of God's covenanted but unconventional love!

†

Third Joyful Mystery
JESUS IS BORN
Matthew 1:18—2:11, Luke 2:1–20

"...and wrapped him in bands of cloth..."
(Luke 2:7)

People often complain when Christmas decorations are displayed before Thanksgiving. I understand, but I cannot empathize.

154

I regret that the Christmas story is limited to one day, December 25, or even to weeks in advance. In my most exacting moments, I do not want Christmas *Day*. I do not want to cram into one day a story so rich and inexhaustible. Boldly, I have sung Christmas songs in August. The entirety of the gospel is told in the Christmas story, and it would be sad were we to limit these stories to one day. Surely, they fit into the Advent season when we celebrate the many ways of God's coming to us, but then, Advent is never to be forgotten, just as the ministry of John the Baptist is never done. Because of the mysteries of the annunciation and visitation, we who pray the Rosary are already launched into the celebration every time we pick up the beads, with the full expectation that the whole of the good news will be reflected in the birth story of Jesus.

By *not* including the story of Jesus' birth, the evangelist John enriches what Matthew and Luke have given us. John broadens considerably the perspective of the birth of a child with his own rendering: "The Word became flesh" (1:14). John's words are a comprehensive summing up of the gospel message. From the beginning, he anticipated the missionary outcome of the synoptic story of Matthew and Luke, and thus contributed mightily to the Christian movement. In Jesus, God laid claim to the whole of creation. By beginning his text with an echo of the very beginning of the Book of Genesis, John ensures that we will not miss the implications. What verve!

Every Gospel begins with building the context for the ministry of Jesus. Mark did so with a pastiche of biblical texts and with John the Baptist in the garb of the ancient prophets, outlandish diet included. Like John, Mark did not give us an infancy narrative (1:1–8). It could be that there were still tensions in the

Markan community over how to integrate the family of Jesus into the early Christian movement. Already evident in Mark is a willingness to interpret the family of Jesus away from blood relationship to models of discipleship (Mark 3:31–35). Jesus' family are those doing the will of God, a new model that would later be reinterpreted by Luke in terms of hearing and doing the word of God (Luke 8:19–21).

Readers of the infancy narratives of Matthew and Luke share the difficulty of keeping stories separate and hearing each Gospel on its own terms. Ever since the production and distribution of the *Diatessaron* of Tatian of Syria in the early centuries, wherein the four Gospels were conflated into one grand story, there has been a struggle to hear each evangelist in terms of his own presentation, concerns, and religious modeling. Today, we are more sensitive than in the days of Tatian to the advantages of comparing and contrasting the ways that the individual evangelists handle the various traditions.

Luke has the lion's share of Christmas iconography. The effect is that our focus is drawn to Luke, but we cannot lose track of the contributions of Matthew. At Christmas, I often sit in reflection at the crèche and strive to sort out the elements. For instance, I do not want to see the arrival of the magi before Epiphany. That is about as much representation Matthew's presentation gets in the crèche but certainly not his only contribution to the Christmas story. Attention to the liturgical readings gives a more rounded view of both Matthew and Luke. As I have noted earlier, just as Mary and Elizabeth appreciated each other's gifts, I like to think that Matthew and Luke would not only have seen the strength in each other's gifts but also the complementarity of their presentations. For Luke no less than for

Matthew, the message was presented in the characterization of people's lives. The early churches awaited eagerly the gift of the evangelists' narrative portraits of Jesus and of the people whose lives he touched.

Yes, the differences between Matthew and Luke are apparent. For example, each took a different approach to a conundrum faced by the early movement, testified to in John 7:41: "But some asked, 'Surely the Messiah does not come from Galilee, does he? Has not the scripture said that the Messiah is descended from David and comes from Bethlehem, the village where David lived?'" Matthew used an angel, seen in a dream, to lead Joseph through a series of actions in the first two chapters, from marrying the pregnant Mary to settling in the town of Nazareth. Each action is explained in terms of being done "to fulfill what had been written by the prophet," and then each is followed by an appropriate Old Testament verse. After the flight to Egypt, Joseph finally returns to Israel, and is again warned of danger in a dream. So he "went away to the district of Galilee. There he made a home in a town called Nazareth, so that what had been spoken through the prophets might be fulfilled, 'He will be called a Nazorean'" (2:23). Although that exact passage—"He will be called a Nazorean"—has never been satisfactorily identified by modern readers, Matthew concludes his presentation on the point. Thus he answers the conundrum as part of his intention to show that in Jesus the scriptures were being fulfilled.

Luke, on the other hand, builds his answer to the Bethlehem-Nazareth conundrum in reference to a demand of the Roman Empire that all return to their hometowns to be registered in a census (2:1–5). In place of quotations from scriptures, Luke honors the continuity in the story of salvation by giving narrative expositions: "Joseph also went up from the town of Nazareth in Galilee to Judea, to the city of David called Bethlehem, because he descended from the house and family of David. He went to be registered with Mary, to whom he was engaged and who was expecting a child" (2:4–5). Luke's reference to the story of salvation is framed by reference to the Roman Empire and the family of Caesar (2:1, 3:1). We see Jesus' family in relation to the family of Caesar. Some will say that Luke has a grudge against the Empire; others will call him the theologian of the Empire. I see Luke as losing no time in subtly reinterpreting what it means to belong to any organized structure and how to find a new identity in the church as missionary family of Jesus. He relates the birth of Jesus to wider social dimensions in which the early movement was making its way.

Luke tells the actual birth of Jesus in two verses; the circumstances under which it took place run another nineteen verses (birth, 2:6–7; circumstances, 2:1–5, 8–20). Reading the footnotes at this point in one's Bible is enlightening because the reader comes to see the many allusions in Luke's text that relate to the wider biblical picture. Thus, even in this simple, seemingly uncomplicated story of a birth—"There was no place for them in the inn"—Luke is missionary from beginning to end. Can you belong to an empire and have no place to have a child?

"There was no place for them in the inn...." This establishes a central tension in the birth narrative and anticipates the later rejection of Jesus. On his visit to the synagogue in his hometown, Jesus interpreted the scriptures in favor of the undesirable outsider, and then proceeded to claim biblical precedent for this outrageous rereading of Isaiah the prophet (Luke 4:16–30). This inclusion of the outsider is Luke's image of church. It is disturbing. In Luke, the church never becomes an entity unto itself; it is always pulsating with the energy of the claim of God upon the whole of our human lives. The good news will be in favor of the outsider, refinding the center from the margins, in an attitude of inclusion. In what I call the pastoral seminar in Luke 10, future missionaries are imbued with this attitude of drawing from the margins. But the reader does not have to wait till chapter 10—nor even chapter 4, Jesus' inaugural reading in the synagogue—to sense the missionary impulse. To reread the infancy narrative is to become aware of all the storytelling devices—for example, flashback, foreshadowing, dialogue—that extend the layers of metaphor that enliven Luke's presentation of Jesus' vision of community. A reader may assume that Luke wrote the infancy narrative, his overture to the Gospel and Acts, *after* he had completed writing the entire manuscript. Luke's details of the birth of Jesus act to draw the stranger in from the margins, a program that takes the community to the center of the Empire.

Pulled in from the margins, Jesus is placed in the animal trough in swaddling clothes: "She wrapped him in bands of cloth, and laid him in a manger, because there was no place for them in the inn" (Luke 2:7). In American social history, accounts of newborns cradled in cupboard drawers suggest hard-edged practicality and resourcefulness: Use what you have at hand. The child will grow and the drawer can be put back. Inventiveness and frugality are the ways of the immigrant and the poor and here, in a daring image, the model of God's kingly claim upon us. Again, Luke is content with an allusion to the biblical tradition. Wisdom 7:4–6 reads: "I was nursed with care in swaddling clothes. / For no king has had a different beginning of existence; / there is for all one entrance into life, and one way out." If necessity is the mother of invention, it is wise to tailor one's wants to one's needs and there will be plenty for all. Swaddling clothes and regal wisdom, it's hard to better this paradox!

Luke mentions the clothes a second time when the angels appear to the shepherds: "This will be a sign for you: you will find a child wrapped in bands of cloth and lying in a manger" (2:12). The swaddling clothes, now the attire of the new king, will be the sign to the shepherds, an important element in their call-story, that they should not fear their nocturnal visitors. The very first ones to be called to missionary life are the shepherds: angelic appearance, experience of glory, and the onslaught of fear! And then there is the reassuring word: "I am bringing you good news of great joy for all the people." Not unlike the angelic annunciation to Mary, this one deftly wrought sentence sums up the whole Christian creed: "To you is born this day in the city of David a Savior who is the Messiah, the Lord." Never have two templates, God's deed and human need, come together so beautifully: God's deed, in the word *Lord*, and the human need of a savior, *this day*. As the image of the swaddling clothes opens out in an allusion to the new kingdom and the fulfillment of the promise of a messiah, the angel's voice cedes to an angelic chorus: "Glory to God in the highest heaven, and on earth peace among those whom he favors" (2:14).

The person who nurtures his or her praying the Rosary by reading Luke will recognize the word *today* as often used by the evangelist, and will immediately follow the lead of shepherds and angels in praising God. They will be joined by many others praising God daily. Take, as an example, the man who, both Samaritan and leper, was healed by Jesus and looks forward to a new life praising God (17:11–19). Or take the repentant thief who hears the word *today* as he never heard it before: "Today you will be with me in Paradise" (23:43). This band, then, of unlikely heroes forms the community praising God in the temple in Jerusalem at the completion of the story (24:53).

Luke never lets go of his message. He knows the template of our lives. He will consistently present the claim of God upon our lives in symbols and images that grasp us in our ordinariness, even when he has the most extraordinary things to share. The growth of the Christian movement shows how successful his strategy was. No, not his alone, but he did write a very large part of the movement's first literature. And he had the talents and skills necessary at that time to communicate the message. Was he not like the shepherds in their task of telling the story of glorifying and praising God? But that proclamation must always come from the lips of a community of simple people, also glorifying and praising God.

Between reference to the evangelism of the shepherds (2:18) and mention of their belonging to a community of praise (2:20), Luke places Mary in her deepest moment of contemplation: "Mary treasured all these words and pondered them in her heart" (2:19). This depiction of Mary is a master stroke. Mary has heard from the shepherds the message of the angels: "Glory to God in the highest heaven, / and on earth peace among those whom he favors" (2:14). The intended meaning of "those whom he favors" must be, as the Revised Standard Version footnote indicates, "those whom God has chosen in accord with his good will." This is not a limitation on the divine benevolence. God's favor rests on all humankind without restriction.

Between this angelic message at the birth of Jesus and the speech of Jesus beginning his public ministry, a significant connection is made. The theme of God's favor returns as "the year of the Lord's favor" (4:19). God's favor to humans is spelled out in the imagery of a jubilee year recalling the symbol of a time of freeing people from debts and giving them a new life. The necessity of Jesus' life of suffering, death, and resurrection in his work as Savior, Messiah, and Lord is anticipated in the good favor of God to humankind announced by the angels. Linking the favor of God and peace on earth, within the angelic song of glory, dramatically lays out the mission of Jesus. In the tradition, these two elements have been interwoven in many ways, though the sequence is clearly recognized: glory to God, then peace on earth through the experience of God's favor. These elements inspire and give direction to a year of freedom and reconciliation. Mary needs to look no further than Joseph for one on whom God's favor rests.

"In a dream..."
(Matt 1:20)

By contrast, Matthew's presentation of the infancy narrative focuses on Joseph. By contemplating his responses to some very unusual circumstances, we bring together, in a creative tension, templates of his life and ours. In discussing Joseph's handling of Mary's pregnancy, we referred to him as "just." He is said to be righteous, which means law-abiding, because he interprets with creativity and daring the claims that the Torah (law) make upon him. Mary, his fiancée, is found to be with child before they have come together as husband and wife. Through the irony of Matthew's storytelling, the reader knows what Joseph doesn't: that the child to be born has been conceived in Mary through the Holy Spirit. "Unwilling to expose her to public disgrace," Joseph decides to divorce her quietly (1:19). Instead of subjecting Mary to the possibility of being publicly punished, if not stoned—although we are unsure of the exact punishment in that particular epoch—Joseph interprets the law in her favor. For this he is known as "righteous."

Matthew revisits the question of righteousness later in his Gospel. There we may ask the question: In Matthew's judgment, is Joseph's conduct a model for the work of interiorization for which Jesus calls in the Sermon on the Mount? There Jesus says, "Do not think that I have come to abolish the law or the prophets. I have come not to abolish but to fulfill" (5:17). In constructing the words of Jesus, Matthew leaves the verbs *abolish* and *fulfill* without objects. If we supply the missing objects of these verbs, we come close to Matthew's understanding of righteousness. Normally, in the first Gospel, the verb *fulfill* goes with mention of prophets. Therefore, I understand the phrase as "I have come not to abolish the law, but to fulfill the prophets." The meaning, I suggest, is "in how I fulfill the prophets, I will reinterpret the law." This meaning, I suggest further, is confirmed in the Sermon on the Mount where we read the six great (re)interpretations, often dubbed "antitheses," on anger, adultery, divorce, oaths, retaliation, and love of enemies. Jesus shows a great freedom at times abolishing, but more often, interiorizing the observance of the law. All of this is introduced by the saying in 5:20: "I tell you, unless your righteousness surpasses that of the scribes and Pharisees you will never enter the kingdom of heaven." In interpreting the law in favor of Mary, Joseph's righteousness surpasses that of the Pharisees, and he is claimed by God's righteousness.

If, on the one hand, Matthew was prepared to model righteousness in the person of Joseph, who interpreted the law in favor of relationship, on the other hand, he presents Joseph as the one who carries the imagination of Israel in a dream. The annunciation to Joseph is a dream sequence. So also is the command to protect the child and his mother against Herod, and likewise, to bring them back (2:13, 19). Finally, the eventual set-tling down in Galilee is also communicated in a dream (2:22).

The person praying the Rosary brings to the contemplation of this mystery the memory of another Joseph, another dreamer, in the book of Genesis, who is also remembered as the great provider (37:5). When the Egyptians clamored for food during a famine, Pharaoh said, "Go to Joseph" (41:55). In Leuven, Belgium, along-side the national shrine to St. Joseph, where thousands come to pray in the month of March, there is a garden with those words, "Go to Joseph," displayed over the gate. The same words appear in countless churches dedicated to this man. Many struggling fami-lies have found consolation in this command to go to Joseph, the good provider who dreams. So often in life we divide the two roles, thinking that there are those who make the hard practical decisions about providing for others, and then there are the dreamers whose intuitions we may be slow to trust. But Joseph holds the two roles together in righteousness, living out concretely God's claim upon him. I believe that Matthew intended these many aspects to show through the story, but he must have known that it would take many readings to come to an adequate appreciation of Joseph.

Healthy role models of masculinity are difficult to come by. In recent times, much has been written to present models of a Christian male: who he is, how he cares for his family, how he expresses intimacy and warmth, how he projects power and leader-ship. Each culture constructs gender models. The struggle of many a teenager in the crucible of high school education is to find oneself and not fall prey to others' stereotypes. The struggle expands when certain cultural expectations, mostly unexamined, are foisted upon people in different ways, many unrecognized but nonetheless damaging. One may think immediately of movies and print media, as well as video games in the local mall. Church culture has played a not insignificant part in promoting patriarchal mindsets, seen, for instance, in pastoral practice, prejudicially siding with the male in many emotionally troubled marriages. A single man is often put on the defensive over his marital status, and if he chooses celibacy for the sake of the gospel, his life is tersely regarded as a waste. To these stigmatizing templates of modern culture, Joseph offers what must seem to be heroic counter-intuitions.

Joseph, who did not press his rights and who provided for his family, is an altogether challenging figure. The story of salvation, in fulfillment of the scriptures, unfolding through actions often taken in the face of fear and prejudice, could not have gone forward were it not for the likes of Joseph, portrayed by Matthew as a righteous man who, for instance, by his obedience foiled the attempts of Herod to destroy the child. Obviously, Matthew is writing his Gospel to assure his readers that the Christian movement is God's faithful fulfillment of all the promises made to Israel. So the protagonist is God, and the faithful servant is Joseph or others who will be like him. If the story of our salvation is "promise made, promise fulfilled" by an all-faithful and caring God, the fragile tissue of our lives whereby *we* make and keep promises is modeled for us by Joseph. We are invited by Joseph to dream, and so I dream of a world where promises made are promises fulfilled. How different the world would be! Fidelity is such a beautiful experience, and the well-being of so many children is utterly dependent on the selfless fulfillment of promises made. The person praying the Rosary can certainly enter into this dream and, in fidelity, recommit to all the promises made.

Keeping promises doesn't mean that we do not reinterpret. Life changes, but a reinterpreted promise needs to be justified, that is, made righteous through communication, explanation, and negotiation. A promise to bury a parent's body in a given location may not be possible. Can the change be explained and negotiated? A promise never to relocate because of work opportunities may have to be discussed, prayed over, and genuinely discerned. We are never intended to have full knowledge of all eventualities when we promise, but can we treat with respect those to whom we promised by sitting down, dialoguing, and renegotiating within the commitment made?

Hope is born of promises made and promises kept. The virtue of hope is trusting, on the strength of having already experienced God's fidelity, that God will be faithful to God's promises. Hope is action, always related to faith in the God who raised Jesus to glory. How to live in response to such a faithful God was the challenge to the community. They searched for models. For many, Joseph, a man of action, an intuitive provider, was a hands-down favorite!

†

Fourth Joyful Mystery

JOSEPH AND MARY PRESENT JESUS

Luke 2:22–38

"...for the falling and the rising..."
(Luke 2:34)

My mother was "churched." Some days after my birth, when she could move around safely, she went to church to thank

God for the birth of her child and to be readmitted to the community of praise. To interpret the ceremony, we go not to the taboo on sex that no doubt played a part in the thinking behind the ceremony, but rather to where such a taboo may have come from. To give birth was to enter a field of awesome sacredness, and one needed a reentry rite to resume life in the *secula*, the world. Popularly, the ceremony was known as purification, and the feast of Jesus' presentation in the temple was often known as the purification of Mary. This mystery of the Rosary invites a close reading of the text of Luke, from whom alone we have an account. The presentation will always be aligned with the purification of Mary in the sense suggested above.

This mystery of the Rosary is drawn from what is called Luke's "special source," meaning a source known to Luke and either not known or not used by Matthew or Mark. Luke is evidently constructing his own scenarios. One indication is how Luke clearly draws from the available language of the law on the purification rite rather than on an actual incident as it took place in historical time. The reference to the law that states the mother will bring a pigeon or a turtledove establishes that Joseph and Mary were law-abiding Jews (Exod 13:2, 12; Lev 12:1–8). In retrospect, every detail told about Jesus finds legitimation in a rereading of the older text.

Later in Luke, after Jesus begins his ministry, he returns to his hometown of Nazareth, unrolls the scroll of Isaiah, and proclaims that the scripture had been fulfilled that day in him (Luke 4:16–21). All were amazed and asked, "Is this Joseph's son?" (v. 22). Jesus answers by saying that a prophet is not honored in his hometown and that Elijah and Elishu worked their miracles not at home but for the widow Zarephath in the Gentile land of

Sidon; and for Naaman, a commander in the land of Syrian (1 Kgs 17:8–24 and 2 Kgs 5:1–14, respectively). Because these two had no connection with the prophets, their testimony was more convincing. Luke longed to introduce two such witnesses to Jesus as the Messiah, and he found them in Anna, a prophetess, and in Simeon, a righteous and devout man (Luke 2:22–38). Thus, the presentation of Jesus in the temple is really a way to honor all who awaited the redemption of Jerusalem.

In each of the three introductory verses, we read of the Holy Spirit variously acting on Simeon and, by extension, on Anna (2:25–27). In Simeon and Anna, Luke has two well-trusted, "from the beginning…eye-witnesses and servants of the word" (Luke 1:2) as he takes on the task of portraying the Jerusalem-to-Rome plot construction of the Christian story. Within Luke's text Simeon precedes Anna. Here I choose, in deference to the Jerusalem-to-Rome direction of the Christian movement, to hear from Anna first because her concern is with Jerusalem, and then from Simeon who is concerned with openness to the Gentiles.

With Anna, Luke introduces what will be one of his favorite social roles, that of the widow (2:36–38). He knows well that in his society widows had *no* social status and is aware of the care of widows within the arrangement of the Christian community (see 1 Tim 5:3–16). Breaking down boundaries, Luke is challenging the culture of his times. The template is still relevant today where, in some parts of the world, a bereaved woman still suffers a stigma upon the death of her husband. Luke does not skimp in describing Anna's lineage and status: daughter of Phanuel, of the tribe of Asher, eighty-four years old, having been widowed seven years after her marriage. Like Mary, she is a prophetess. We have no direct language from Anna but an indication in the text that she spoke to those around her. Her concerns find voice over the spectrum of Luke's plot. She is one of the unforgettable characters to grace the scroll. The whole journey of Jesus to Jerusalem is anticipated in her contemplative demeanor and in her prayer and fasting. John the Baptist can only learn from her in this regard.

Anna is a stand-in for the *anawim*, the poor of Israel, the ones whose lives and spirituality are open to receive the gift of God. In a gospel where particular emphasis is placed on the women who accompanied Jesus to Jerusalem, Anna the prophetess stands as a rebuke to the exclusion of women from the affairs of this world and from the matters of religion. Does she intuit that over the centuries many of her widowed companions will keep the prayers going, the ageless contemplation of the beads, the emotive connection with the deeper story unfolding before us? When Jesus will later give a parable about the necessity to pray always without becoming weary, Luke turns to an example of a persistent widow who will not take no for an answer (18:1–8). The example of Anna's many years of worshiping day and night come to mind when we hear that parable. In Anna's prayer, God found faith on earth, a willingness to receive the redemption of Jerusalem (18:8, 2:38, respectively).

Powerful stories sometimes contain the widest gaps. The reader's imagination goes beyond the text to fill in what's missing, and thus the story is enriched. Take, for instance, the apocryphal conjecture that Joseph died early and left Mary a widow to accompany Jesus alone to Jerusalem. The idea is perhaps fanciful, but within the text of Luke, there would be deep sympathy for a widowed mother. This sympathy comes through, for example, in the situation of the widow of Nain, whose only son died and who is resuscitated by Jesus (7:11–17). The chorus that erupts in response to this connects marvelously with the spirituality of Anna. The text reads: "Fear seized all of them; and they glorified God, saying, 'A great prophet has risen among us,' and 'God has looked favorably on his people'" (7:16). Then there is the enigmatic widow who gives her all as Jesus passes into the city of his destiny (21:1–4). Like Jesus, she gives not from what won't be missed (surplus wealth) but from *all* that she has to live on. Luke's point is that we should not only be good to widows but also value them. In Luke's depiction, widows carry an openness to the gift of life that Jesus is bringing. Call that gift visitation, call it redemption, call it liberation, call it justice, call it peace.

Anna is calling for Jubilee because she epitomizes loss and vulnerability. The person praying the Rosary is in solidarity with Anna's prayer. He or she relates to the hungers of our modern world in the opening years of the twenty-first century. These vulnerabilities may be the existential hunger for meaning in the economically prosperous world, or the concrete hunger for food in the economically ravaged world, a plight often made more painful by ethnic cleansing. Anna is surrendering the hungers of this life to the fidelity of God to deliver Jerusalem. If we heard Anna's words, would they not have echoed the hopeful mantra of the impoverished widow of Zarephath: "The jar of meal will not be emptied, and the jug of oil will not fail, until the day that the Lord sends rain on the earth" (1 Kgs 17:14).

Anna's words focus on Jerusalem, Simeon's words on the mission to the Gentiles (Luke 2:29–32). Simeon, like Anna, awaited the deliverance of Jerusalem, but his missionary horizon is expressed by pairing two verses from the prophet of consolation, Isaiah. "A light for revelation to the Gentiles" comes from

Isaiah 42:6, and from 46:13 we have "glory to your people Israel." When Simeon says, "For my eyes have seen your salvation, / which you prepared in the presence of all peoples," he anticipates the words of John the Baptist: "And all flesh shall see the salvation of God" (Luke 3:6). John's words also echo Isaiah 40:5 and 52:10. Simeon's vision ("my eyes have seen your salvation…") may even be said to reverberate, for the modern reader, the claim in John the Evangelist's gospel summation: "The Word became flesh" (John 1:14).

Sandwiched between the words of Simeon and the action of Anna is a warning addressed to Mary to which the reader of Luke will often return: "A sword will pierce your own soul too" (Luke 2:35). Indeed, Christian iconography often depicts Mary's heart, the locus of her inner thoughts, as being pierced. Because the previous phrase is "the inner thoughts of many will be revealed," we wonder: Does the text include Mary in the many whose inner thoughts will be revealed? Is Mary exempt from personal struggle, or is she one with the struggles of all disciples?

On the one hand, a reader could approach the text on an assumption of personal exemption of Mary from such struggles despite all she experiences. The interpretation would go like this: Her son's mission was not only to preach salvation but to embrace the rejection of his own words of life and consolation. She cannot be indifferent to the rejection of her son, and her own heart will know many sorrows. How could the heart of the mother of the Suffering Servant be untouched? However, in this approach, despite her solidarity with the sorrows of the mission of Jesus, Mary is personally exempt from the troubles that Jesus, as a sign to be contradicted, causes in peoples' hearts. In this approach, Mary's sorrows would be real but without struggle.

On the other hand, is Mary herself beset with struggles of her own; namely, the struggle to believe? The text implies that her whole person, as mother and disciple, will also be claimed by the rise and fall of her son, with the consequence that "the inner thoughts of many will be revealed" when they stand against the sign that is Jesus. Is Mary among the "many"? Often in Luke, an action of Jesus throws the disciples into disarray (5:22; 6:8; 9:46, 47). The word *revealed* is in the passive voice and opens the reflection that God reveals the inner disarray in which people find themselves when confronted with Jesus.[5] Mary, although mother of the Messiah, was nonetheless a disciple. She herself will hear her blessedness as mother redefined in terms of discipleship: "Hear the word of God and obey it" (Luke 11:27–28). This redefinition is echoed in the later warning that Christians, because of their faith in Jesus, will struggle with conflict in their families to whom Jesus brought not peace but division (Luke 12:49–53; note that in the Matthean parallel 10:34–36 the word *sword* is used). The struggle is brought back to the greeting of the angel at the annunciation when Mary "was much perplexed by his words" (1:29). "And a sword will pierce your own soul too." These two verses may in fact indicate that Mary was not exempt and that she too had her own struggles in accepting Jesus.

For the person praying the Rosary, this way of hearing the words of Simeon—namely, that Mary was not without her own struggles to believe—may be a shock. Upon reflection, however, this presentation of Mary as disciple is profoundly strengthening. The template of our lived experience of coming to faith in Jesus is set alongside the template of Mary's similar journey. Mary is not outside the *need* of the saving power of

Jesus, although she experienced that grace in anticipation. Neither are *we* outside the need of God's saving grace, nor should we ever regret that we are in constant need of grace. An old spirituality of perfectionism still stalks us, saying that we should *not* have to need God's grace. How much better is it to image ourselves as Mary, called to take our place within the graced community of the great story of salvation than, as lone individuals before God, to burden our souls with the attempt to be perfect? We do not have to pit our individual salvation over against that of the group but rather we may accept our vocation within the community as salvation. The greatest "falling and… rising" we will ever experience is taking our place in the unfolding of God's design of saving love for all humankind and all creation.

Balancing these concerns—individual and private, group and public, but always deeply personal—is achieved by telling a call-story, a literary convention we have come to appreciate already on a number of occasions. In Mary's case, the call-story shows her taking her place within the unfolding of God's design and at the same time having a template in which to work out the questions of her own inner "thoughts." Mary may not be mentioned in the final chapter of Luke's Gospel but her example of discipleship, once found in her questioning the angel at the annunciation, is found in the question of Jesus, as Risen Lord, to the assembled disciples in Jerusalem: "Why are you frightened, and why do doubts arise in your hearts?" (24:38). On the strength of this "why?" we turn to the final joyful mystery and the question about Jesus that gives ultimate meaning to the Rosary.[6]

†

Fifth Joyful Mystery
JESUS LOST AND FOUND IN THE TEMPLE IN JERUSALEM
Luke 2:41–52

"Why?…Did you not know…?"
(Luke 2:49)

To put it lightly, bringing up Jesus was no picnic. Already twice in Luke's infancy narrative, Mary is said to have reflected in her heart on her experiences of the events unfolding around her (2:19, 51). The first time was after the visit of the shepherds. The second time was after the episode in the temple when "the boy Jesus stayed behind in Jerusalem, but his parents did not know it." When the parents and child finally catch up with each other, the tense and terse conversation ricochets between two *whys:* "Why have you treated us like this?"…"Why were you searching for me?" The first why gets expanded: "Your father and I have been searching for you with great anxiety." The second why is expanded by another question: "Did you not know that I must be in my Father's house?" or, as the footnote says, in an alternative translation from the Greek, "Did you not know that I must be about my Father's interests?" The second possibility is to be preferred because "work" or "interests" include the Father's house, meaning the temple, among other matters. In fact, the temple is particularly important in Luke's presentation of Jesus but precisely as the place where Jesus does the Father's business. The temple gets reinterpreted out of the relationship that Jesus has with his Father, God. That relationship also reinterprets Jesus' relationship with his family, now composed of those who *hear* and *do* God's word. The contrast between "your father" on the lips of Mary, meaning Joseph, and "my Father" on the lips of Jesus, meaning God, enriches this narrative as one of the more challenging reversals of expectations in Christian life.

No matter what commentators may say about the distinct historical feasibility of Jesus going to Jerusalem, and, furthermore, at this age in his life, the importance of this exchange does not lie in historical likelihood but its placement as the conclusion of Luke's infancy narrative. In this bridge text between infancy and ministry, Luke introduces the understanding of the prophetic necessity laid on the life of Jesus, the *why* of his life: "I must be about my Father's interests." Luke, unlike Mark, does not hold off to the end of his story to confess that Jesus is the Son of God. Rather, he begins with the confession and shows in what way Jesus is the Son of God. Jesus bears the necessity of God to save us. Of course, it is not enough to claim this without counterbalancing it with God's response to this faithful service of Jesus, his resurrection. This is the great atonement; namely, Jesus is "at-one" with the Father's desire to save all humankind. It is this "at-one-ment" with the will of his Father that reveals Jesus as the Son obedient in fulfilling the redemption of Jerusalem.[7]

Mary and Joseph are the first disciples to learn this message of obedience of Jesus' sonship. Yet his sonship is not resolved within the story of his being lost and found as a child in Jerusalem. Over the whole course of Luke's Gospel, and, especially when Jesus teaches in the temple area after being tempted in the desert, Luke is leading us to a conviction of the early community about Jesus. Jesus' first visit to the temple as a child anticipates his ministry there after his regal entry into Jerusalem (19:28—20:44). Arguably, in terms of plot, the most developed aspect of his visit as a youth are the two verses devoted to it: "After three days they found him in the temple, sitting in the midst of the teachers, listening to them and asking them questions. And all who heard him were astounded at his understanding and his answers" (vv. 46–47). This is a convincing example of the introductory statement in the transitional verse 40: "The child grew and became strong, filled with wisdom; and the favor of God was with him."

Jesus' teaching in Jerusalem (19:28—20:44) is common to the two other Synoptic Gospels, Mark and Matthew. The question asked by Mary—"Why have you treated us like this?" (2:48)—foreshadows the question that the Pharisees and elders ask, when Jesus begins his teaching in the temple: "By what authority are you doing these things? Who is it who gave you this authority?" (20:2). The Pharisees' shift from *"what authority"* to *"who gave you this authority"* is significant because it casts light on the relationship between Jesus and God. Jesus responds with a similar question about John the Baptist: "Did the baptism of John come from heaven, or was it of human origin?" (20:4). Aspects eminently true of Jesus come to light: He is of heavenly origin and he too like John is a prophet (20:1–8).

After this exchange follow several episodes that contribute to an overall answer to the Pharisees' question, "Who is it who gave you this authority?" The first is the parable of the tenant farmers (20:9–19), which tells of a plot to kill the heir, the son who has come to receive the inheritance. Then Jesus, standing in the temple, says, "The stone that the builders rejected has become the cornerstone" (Luke 20:17, citing Ps 118:22).

In the next episode the Pharisees ask, "Is it lawful for us to pay taxes to the emperor, or not?" (Luke 20:22). The following verse explicitly mentions the "craftiness" with which the question is meant to trap Jesus into a choice between the religious unlawfulness of giving tribute to Caesar and the secular unlawfulness of not paying taxes. Jesus asks for a denarius, and then asks "Whose head and whose title [literally, *icon*] does it bear?... Then give to the emperor the things that are the emperor's, and to God the things that are God's" (20:24–25). The one question and answer sort out not only the claims made by Caesar but also the claims made by the one who bears God's icon. A further question is implied: "Whose icon, whose image, do *I* bear? Do *I* belong to God?" This contributes new language to answering the question, "Who is it who gave you this authority?" In the language of our contemplation, we would ask the Pharisees: Who has claim over you, whose icon do you bear, in whose image are you made? Or in the language of this scene in Luke: Do you belong to the one who has come to claim the inheritance?

The next episode concerns the Sadducees, who did not believe in resurrection, belabored as they were with models of resuscitation and return to this earthly life (20:27–40). The Sadducees present to Jesus the extreme case of one woman married to seven brothers, and then ask whose wife she will be at the resurrection. How Jesus presents God in response to this question adds more to the picture of how Jesus is the Son: "Now he is God not of the dead, but of the living, for to him all of them are alive" (20:38). In an inclusive covenanted understanding of Jesus as Risen Lord, he is the son of the God of the Patriarchs, to whom all are alive.

This response about the God of the resurrection prepares us for the concluding scene when it is Jesus' turn to ask a question: "How can they say that the Messiah is David's son?" (20:41–44). No doubt this was a common question in the early community of Jewish Christians. Did the discussion begin with the promise about the son of David and lead to the expectation of the messiah on the grounds of natural descent? Or did the discussion begin with the lived experience of the actual Messiah and call him son of David because of the experience of the presence of the Risen Lord, that the resurrection is God's fulfillment of the promises of inheritance made to David? Quoting from Psalm 110, Jesus expands his question: "For David himself says in the book of Psalms, // 'The Lord said to my Lord, / "Sit at my right hand..."' // David thus calls him Lord; so how can he be his son?" (Luke 20:42–44). Jesus is Lord, Messiah, son of David, because he is son of God, faithfully carrying out the messianic necessity of God's love, to save the world that is laid upon him and that he lovingly and willfully embraces. "Child, why have you treated us like this?" and "Who is it who gave you this authority?"—both questions are answered in the experience of the Risen Lord.[8]

This composite response to the question of Jesus' authority comes sparklingly clear in the speech of Peter in the Acts of the Apostles (2:14–36) and notably in the concluding verse: "Therefore let the whole house of Israel know with certainty that God has made him both Lord and Messiah, this Jesus whom you crucified." The words *whom you crucified* indicate how Jesus must be about his Father's work. What Jesus asks the disciples on the road to Emmaus reveals the why: "Was it not necessary that the Messiah should suffer these things and then enter into his glory?" (Luke 24:26). His teaching in Jerusalem shows that Jesus has been given the authority—that is, the necessity, prophetic and messianic—to die and to be raised as a way to inherit the promise of the Father, now no longer just a city but the Holy Spirit in whom to fashion a new people!

In the anxiety of Mary and Joseph about Jesus lost in Jerusalem, Luke opened up a whole process of reflection on how Jesus is the Son of the Father. As if to give an even more elaborate answer than already shared in the Gospel, Luke in the Acts of the Apostles (7:1–60) gives us the speech of Stephen. Stephen shows how Jesus in his relationship with God is where God wants to be worshiped. This is but a variant on a fundamental issue in all of human seeking: Where and how does God give access to Godself? Where does God want us to approach God? Only God can give access to God. So then, to whom has God given the power to give access? And how is such a one related to God? Even the confession that the emissary of God is God's Son invites yet another question: How is he son?

Close to the end of Stephen's speech, he asks, "Which of the prophets did your ancestors not persecute?" (Acts 7:52). Filled with the Holy Spirit, Stephen contemplates "the glory of God and Jesus standing at the right hand of God" (v. 55), and in this vision is the whole story of how God gives access to Godself in Jesus, the son of Man, he who lived and died as a prophet among us. Earlier, Stephen said that "the Most High does not dwell in houses made with human hands" (7:48). No, we do not worship God on our terms, in houses made by human hands, but on the terms of God the Most High, who raised Jesus, the persecuted prophet, to the glory of God. Stephen leads us back to the words of the angel to Mary: "And now, you will conceive in your womb and bear a son, and you will name him Jesus. He will be great, and will be called the Son of the Most High, and the Lord God will give to him the throne of his ancestor David. He will reign over the house of Jacob forever, and of his kingdom, there will be no end" (Luke 1:31–33). Mary's question, "Child, why have you treated us like this?" and the question of the chief priests, the scribes, and the elders, "Who is it who gave you this authority" have served well to guide our rereading of the story of our salvation as family story of Father and obedient Son.

For the person praying the Rosary, this final mystery opens the whole journey all over again, a journey to be made every day in the life of the Christian. How can one be in this world, sharing the mission of Jesus, and not share in the same necessity to embrace and overcome with love the constant resistance to the message of redeeming love? The kingdom is the claim of God, the necessity of God upon us and that claim is first and foremost placed on the Son, who is totally and completely one with the plans of the Father's love. How do I, in praying the Rosary, embrace the necessity laid upon my life each day? How do I know that that necessity is truly God's necessity? Will I, one day like Stephen, looking at the glory of God, understand my life as lived out of prophetic necessity? Do I identify with Jesus who as Son of God carried the prophetic necessity that God's message of love would be rejected? How can I allow the hope of glory to pervade all my human relationships? Will I, in the midst of my brothers and sisters, in the caravan returning to Jerusalem, seek Jesus, seek to know the meaning of his life, ask every bold question there is, and find in Jesus who learned obedience from what he suffered, Son though he was (Heb 5:8), the access, not made by human hands, to worship the Most High?

AFTERWORD

MARIAN SHRINES

In the reflections offered here, much has been made of contemplation within contemplation, journeys within journeys; surely the experience of a religious pilgrimage focuses and deepens such undertakings as an embrace of what is ultimate. Mary, modestly and from a distance, lived her life in tandem with the journey of Jesus to Jerusalem.

In discussing their more interesting journeys, many people mention Marian shrines. While those in Europe may be better known—Lourdes, Fatima, Knock and Medjugorje, for example—there are many noteworthy ones in America. Two valuable sources of information are Theresa Santa Czaropys and Thomas M. Santa, CSsR, *Marian Shrines of the United States: A Pilgrim's Travel Guide* (Liguori, MO: Liguori Press, 1998). See also Ann María Pineda, "Shrines and Pilgrimages," Peter C. Phan, ed., *Directory on Popular Piety and the Liturgy: Principles and Guidelines Commentary* (Collegeville, MN: Liturgical Press, 2005), 151–62.

For those who pray the Rosary, there may be no Marian shrine in the Americas greater than that of Our Lady of Guadalupe. The journey or pilgrimage there revisits all the reasons why persons have clung to Mary over the centuries. She is the mother who was there for people in times of great cultural deprivation and ruthless colonization, sharing the plight of the poor. If Mary in her Magnificat was the privileged witness of God's reversal of human expectation on behalf of suffering people, the shrine in Mexico is her unique stage. The message of companionship and solidarity claimed there is none other than the emotionally rich content of Catholic social teaching.

APPENDIX

SUMMARY OF THE MYSTERIES

Luminous CLAIM	Sorrowful COUNTER-CLAIM	Glorious ACCLAIM	Joyful PROCLAIM
John baptizes Jesus Matt 3:13–17, Luke 3:10–22 "...to fulfill all righteousness..." God's righteousness as claim to human solidarity	*Gethsemane* Matt 26, Mark 14, Luke 22 "Could you not keep awake one hour?" Temptation as counter-claim	*Resurrection* Matt 28, Mark 16, Luke 24, John 20 "...the one who raised the Lord Jesus..." Acclaiming God who never leaves... abandoned	*Annunciation* Luke 1:26–38 "Greetings, favored one! The Lord is with you." Mary proclaims the greatness of the Lord
Cana John 2:1–11 "Thus did he reveal his glory..." Marriage as claim to glory	*Scourging* Matt 27:26, Mark 15:15, Luke 23:16 "I will therefore have him flogged..." Violence is a lie!	*Ascension* Acts 1:6–12, Eph 4:7–8 "He made captivity itself a captive..." Taking captive the counter-claims	*Visitation* Luke 1:39–56 "...leaped for joy..." Joy discerns claims
Jesus Announces the Reign Matt, Mark, Luke, and John "The kingdom of God is among you..." Kingdom as claim	*Crowning with Thorns* Matt 27:28–31, Mark 15:17–20, John 19:5 "Here is the man..." Endurance in love as ultimate claim to dignity	*Spirit* Acts 2:1–4, 17–21 "People...turning the world upside down..." Spirit co-testifies to God's claim	*Nativity* Luke 2:1–20 "...and wrapped him in bands of cloth..." She remembered
Transformation Matt 17, Mark 9, Luke 9 "They saw his glory..." Yielding to the claim	*Way of the Cross* Matt 27:31–32, Mark 15:20–21, Luke 23:26–32 "...fall on us..." As journeys within journeys	*Assumption* 1 Cor 15:54 "Death...swallowed up in victory" Where he went, she followed	*Presentation* Luke 2:22–38 "...for the falling and the rising..." Mary's first lessons in discipleship
Eucharist Matt 26, Mark 14, Luke 22, John 6 "To whom can we go?" Living the claim	*The Crucifixion* Matt 27, Mark 15, Luke 23, John 19 "You made known to me the ways of life..." Mary as Pietà: Embrace of counter-claim	*Coronation* Matt 6:10, 1 Cor 15 "...on earth as it is in heaven..." The ultimate yield to God's claim upon her	*Finding* Luke 2:41–52 "Why?...Did you not know?" The mystery of God's claim upon your own family

NOTES

INTRODUCTION

1. See the series also in James Martin, SJ, ed., *Awake My Soul: Contemporary Catholics on Traditional Devotions* (Chicago: Loyola Press, 2004). See further Peter C. Phan, ed., *Directory on Popular Piety and the Liturgy: Principles and Guidelines Commentary* (Collegeville, MN: Liturgical Press, 2005). The introduction and eight chapters plus an annotated bibliography offer a commentary on the 2003 document from the Congregation for Divine Worship and the Discipline of the Sacraments. In light of the introduction written by James Empereur, SJ, and his discussion of terminology, it would be correct to refer to the Rosary as a devotion as distinct from a pious exercise, popular piety, or popular religiosity. It is hard to gainsay the relevance of the devotional life today. See further Raymond Jonas, *France and the Cult of the Sacred Heart: An Epic Tale for Modern Times* (Berkeley, CA: University of California Press, 2000); Suzanne K. Kaufman, *Consuming Visions: Mass Culture and the Lourdes Shrine* (Ithaca, NY: Cornell University Press, 2004).

2. John Paul II, *On the Most Holy Rosary [Rosarium Virginis Mariae]* (Washington, DC: USCCB, 2002). Hereafter referred to as "RVM."

3. See Richard Gribble, CSC, *The History and Devotion of the Rosary* (Huntington, IN: Our Sunday Visitor Publishing Division, 1992) for a complete history. Anne Winston-Allen, *Stories of the Rose: The Making of the Rosary in the Middle Ages* (University Park, PA: The Pennsylvania State University Press. 1997) studies the three centuries prior to the Reformation. Only in the fifteenth century did the basic elements that make up the modern Rosary come together: prayer counting, indebtedness to the Psalter, and a life-of-Christ narrative. The history of the Rosary is a social, artistic, and political commentary on the religious life of many

peoples during the many years of its coming together. Winston-Allen, toward the conclusion of her well-documented and compelling study, sadly documents the abuses that came with the quantitative, commodity approach to gaining indulgences attached to the Rosary. Even in the twentieth century, Paul VI had to warn against a mechanical multiplication of prayers. Gribble's work expands the historical perspective up to the present day and shows the Rosary in its role within the Counter-Reformation. This may explain its present eclipse, to cite the expression of Patrick Peyton, CSC, the famed "Rosary priest." See chapter 3 herein, nos. 13 and 14.

4. *RVM*, no. 24.

5. See the history of the study of the Bible in John S. Kselman, SS, and Ronald D. Witherup, SS, "Modern New Testament Criticism," in *New Jerome Biblical Commentary*, Raymond E. Brown SS, Joseph Fitzmyer, SJ, and Roland E. Murphy OCarm, eds. ((New York: Prentice-Hall, 1990), no. 70, 1130–45.

6. "Constitution on the Liturgy Vatican II," in *Documents on the Liturgy* 1963–1979, International Commission for English in the Liturgy (Collegeville, MN: Liturgical Press, 1982), no. 51: "The treasures of the Bible are to be opened up more lavishly, so that a richer share in God's word may be provided for the faithful. In this way a more representative portion of holy Scripture will be read to the people in the course of a prescribed number of years."

7. Sandra M. Schneiders, *The Revelatory Text: Interpreting the New Testament as Sacred Scripture* (San Francisco: Harper, 1991), 44–46.

8. Kevin Irwin, *Models of the Eucharist* (New York/Mahwah, NJ: Paulist Press, 2005). Especially relevant here is his treatment of the Word of God. See also Ernest Falardeau, *A Holy and Living Sacrifice: The Eucharist in Christian Perspective* (Collegeville, MN: Liturgical Press, 1996).

9. These questions represent the mainstay of a modern literary approach. See the discussion of the "world of the text" in Sandra M. Schneiders, "The World of the Text: Witness, Language and the Revelatory Text," *The Revelatory Text: Interpreting the New Testament as Sacred Scripture* (San Francisco: Harper, 1991), 132–56. In *The Interpretation of the Bible in the Church*, by the Pontifical Biblical Commission (Sherbrooke, Quebec:

Editions Paulines, 1994), there is an important statement on the goals of "narrative analysis": "Narrative analysis involves a new way of understanding how a text works. While the historical-critical method considers the text as a 'window' giving access to one or other period (not only to the situation which the story relates but also to that of the community for whom the story is told), narrative analysis insists that the text also functions as a 'mirror,' in the sense that it projects a certain image—a 'narrative world'—which exercises an influence upon readers' perception in such a way as to bring them to adopt certain values rather than others" (45–46).

10. *RVM*, "Contemplating Christ with Mary," nos. 9–17.

11. Jan Lambrecht, SJ, *Second Corinthians,* Sacra Pagina (Collegeville, MN: Liturgical Press, 1999), 49–79.

12. *RVM* no. 13.

13. *RVM* no. 40.

14. Kenneth R. Himes, OFM, *Responses to 101 Questions on Catholic Social Teaching* (New York/Mahwah, NJ: Paulist Press, 2001), 38–39; *Compendium of the Social Doctrine of the Church* (Washington, DC: USCCB, 2005); and Fred Kammer, SJ, *Salted with Fire: Spirituality for the Faithjustice Journey* (New York/Mahwah, NJ: Paulist Press, 1995). But does Catholic social teaching work? Marvin Krier Mitch, *Catholic Social Teaching and Movements* (Mystic, CT: Twenty-Third Publications, 1998), situates Catholic social teaching under several headings, and reviews what is happening on the ground of putting these insights to work. His book is a treasury of insight, in itself a fine example of social history. To explain its purposes, the Catholic Campaign for Human Development published *Principles, Prophecy and a Pastoral Response: An Overview of Modern Catholic Social Teaching* (Washington DC: USCCB, revised 2001). Kevin E. McKenna's *A Concise Guide to Catholic Social Teaching* (Notre Dame, IN: Ave Maria Press, 2002) may stimulate discussion through its concise definitions, overarching concerns, and helpful bibliography. See further McKenna's You *Did It for Me: Care of Your Neighbor as a Spiritual Practice* (Notre Dame, IN: Ave Maria Press, 2005). For advanced study of the issues, see Charles Curran, *Catholic Social Teaching: A Historical, Theological and Ethical Analysis* (Washington, DC: Georgetown University

Press, 2002); and Kenneth R. Himes, OFM, ed., *Modern Catholic Social Teaching: Commentaries and Interpretations* (Washington, DC: Georgetown University Press, 2005). In that book see especially John Donahue, SJ, "The Bible and Catholic Social Teaching," 9–40. And also, Joseph Holland, *Modern Catholic Social Teaching: The Popes Confront the Industrial Age, 1740–1958* (New York/Mahwah, NJ: Paulist Press, 2003).

15. *RVM* no. 19.

16. *RVM* no. 21. For a biblical appreciation of the new Luminous Mysteries, see Roland J. Faley, *The Mysteries of Light: The Bible and the New Luminous Mysteries* (New York/Mahwah, NJ: Paulist Press, 2005).

17. *RVM* no. 21.

18. This proposed arrangement of the mysteries proved helpful in giving retreats on the Rosary. I was able to connect the themes of claim, counter-claim, acclaim, and proclaim as is indicated in the Appendix. See also *RVM* no. 19.

19. The classical description of pathos in the prophets belongs to Abraham Heschel, *The Prophets* (New York: Harper and Row, 1962).

20. Martha Nussbaum, *Upheavals of Thought: The Intelligence of Emotions* (Cambridge: Cambridge University Press, 2001).

21. L. T. Johnson, *Religious Experience in Earliest Christianity: A Missing Dimension in New Testament Studies* (Minneapolis, MN: Fortress, 1998).

22. Francis X. Durrwell, CSsR, *Christ Our Passover: The Indispensable Role of the Resurrection in Our Salvation* (Ligouri, MO: Ligouri Press, 2004). This work is a superb synthesis of his classical works on the resurrection.

23. Paul VI spoke of a bonding in faith that the present community of readers shares with the community for whom this text was their text of faith. This insight on the principle of a co-naturality in faith is echoed in the "reader response," a literary critique of the text. This in turn explores what "text" means. The text is the product of a long process of doing faith and is porous, a medium of communication of the living dynamic word of God, who continues to speak to all people.

24. *Duc in altum,* "put out into the deep" (Luke 5:4), is the motif in John Paul II's apostolic letter, *Novo Millennio Ineunte* (January 6, 2001),

regarding the role of the church in the new millennium, nos. 58–59 (Boston: Pauline, 2001).

1. THE MYSTERIES OF LIGHT

1. *RVM* no. 21.

2. The following quotation by the Lutheran World Federation and the Catholic Church, from the *Joint Declaration on the Doctrine of Justification*, signed October 31, 1999, illustrates not only a balanced understanding of righteousness but shows the fruit of Spirit-filled ecumenical dialogue: "The Catholic understanding also sees faith as fundamental in justification. For without faith, no justification can take place. Persons are justified through baptism as hearers of the word and believers in it. The justification of sinners is forgiveness of sins and being made righteous by justifying grace, which makes us children of God. In justification the righteous receive from Christ faith, hope, and love and are thereby taken into communion with him. *This new personal relation to God is grounded totally on God's graciousness and remains constantly dependent on the salvific and creative working of this gracious God, who remains true to himself, so that one can rely upon him* [emphasis added]. Thus justifying grace never becomes a human possession to which one could appeal over against God. While Catholic teaching emphasizes the renewal of life by justifying grace, this renewal in faith, hope, and love is always dependent on God's unfathomable grace and contributes nothing to justification about which one could boast before God (Rom 3:27)." Pontifical Council for Promoting Christian Unity, Lutheran World Federation, http://www.vatican.va/roman.

3. "Solidarity" is explained in Kenneth R. Himes, OFM, *Responses to 101 Questions on Catholic Social Teaching*, 38–39.

4. William P. Roberts, *Marriage: Sacrament of Hope and Challenge* (Dayton, OH: University of Dayton, 1988). Many married couples, especially in the marriage spirituality group called "Teams of Our Lady," have found this book helpful.

5. In his 2005 World Day of Peace message, John Paul II used a reference to *Gaudium et Spes* embracing interdependent participation, a

constant concern of Catholic social teaching. "The common good therefore demands respect for and the integral promotion of the person and his fundamental rights, as well as respect for and the promotion of the rights of nations on the universal plane. In this regard, the Second Vatican Council observed that 'the increasingly close interdependence gradually encompassing the entire world is leading to an increasingly universal common good...and this involves rights and duties with respect to the whole human race. Every social group must take account of the needs and legitimate aspirations of other groups and the common good of the entire human family' (Pastoral Constitution, *Gaudium et Spes*, §26) The good of humanity as a whole, including future generations, calls for true international cooperation, to which every nation must offer its contribution." From "Overcome Evil with Good," *Origins* 34/29 (2005): 459–62.

6. A recent and very accessible commentary is Richard Clifford's *Psalms 1–72* (Nashville: Abingdon, 2002); and his *Psalms 73–150* (Nashville: Abingdon, 2003).

7. *Dei Verbum* [Document on Revelation], § 19. G. Stanton, and *The Gospels and Jesus* (New York: Oxford University Press, 2002), especially chapter 2, "What Is a Gospel?" 13–36.

8. See Gerd Theissen, *The Miracle Stories of the Early Christian Tradition* (Minneapolis, MN: Fortress, 1983) for the formation of miracle stories.

9. In Psalm 13, four times in six verses that question is asked. The motif is also found in the poignant sufferings of those under the altar in Revelation 6:10, the opening of the fifth seal.

10. Francis J. Moloney, SDB, *The Gospel of John*, Sacra Pagina, series editor Daniel J. Harrington, SJ (Collegeville, MN: Liturgical Press, 1998), 11–13. The ascription of "spiritual gospel" to John is attributed to Clement of Alexandria, second century.

11. Eugene LaVerdiere, *The Eucharist in the New Testament and the Early Church* (Collegeville, MN : Liturgical Press, 1996). The distinction between Lord's Supper and Last Supper shapes this work.

12.   Antony Ceresko, *Introduction to Old Testament Wisdom: A Spirituality of Liberation* (Maryknoll, NY: Orbis, 1999), 178-179.

2. THE SORROWFUL MYSTERIES

1.   On "agony" see Jerome Neyrey, *The Passion According to Luke: A Redaction Study of Luke's Soteriology* (New York/Mahwah, NJ: Paulist Press, 1985), 58–62.

2.   The appreciation of a social interpretation of the text is a fruit of form criticism that studies the actual situations out of which gospel traditions formed. On specific passages, consult Bruce J. Malina and Richard L. Rohrbaugh, *Social Science Commentary on the Synoptic Gospels* (Minneapolis, MN: Fortress, 1992).

3.   See footnote to Luke 22:38, *The Catholic Study Bible,* Donald Senior, CP, gen. ed. (New York: Oxford Press, 1991). This is an enormously helpful work incorporating the text of the New American Bible (NAB) and a Reading Guide totaling more than 500 pages.

4.   See Jeremiah's confessions: 12:1–5, 15:10–21, 17:12–18;,18:18–23, 20:7–18. See also the notes to the above in the NAB and p. RG 316 in the Reading Guide of *The Catholic Study Bible.*

5.   Andrew Sung Park, *The Wounded Heart of God: The Asian Concept of Han and the Christian Doctrine* (Nashville: Abingdon, 1993). What Park presents about *han,* the Asian concept of the harmful effect of sin, could be employed to retrieve, in a social understanding of sin, the Catholic idea of the temporal punishment due to sin. For a recent autobiographical account of one person dealing with the effects of sin, see Laura Blumenfeld's *Revenge* (New York: Simon and Schuster, 2002).

6.   John Paul II, homily, Drogheda, Ireland, October 29, 1979, and the message for World Peace Day, January 1, 2005, no. 4.

7.   See again *The Interpretation of the Bible in the Church,* the Pontifical Biblical Commission (Sherbrooke, Quebec: Editions Paulines, 1994), where rhetorical analysis is the first of the new literary approaches presented.

8. For a history of the interpretation of Christianity's central ethic, see Lisa Sowle Cahill, *Love Your Enemies* (Minneapolis, MN: Fortress, 1994).

9. Drew Christiansen and Walter Grazer, eds., *"And God Saw That It Was Good": Catholic Theology and the Environment* (Washington, DC: United States Catholic Conference, 1996). In this, see especially Anne M. Clifford, "Foundations for a Catholic Ecological Theology of God," 19–46. For many terms used in the current discussion, see Pamela Smith, SSCM, *What Are They Saying About Environmental Ethics?* (New York/Mahwah, NJ: Paulist Press, 1997).

10. The church permits cremation provided that it does not demonstrate a denial of faith in the resurrection of the body. *Catechism of the Catholic Church* (Liguori, MO: Liguori Publications, 1994), no. 2301.

3. THE GLORIOUS MYSTERIES

1. The matter is discussed by Raymond E. Brown, SS, *The Birth of the Messiah,* The Anchor Bible Reference Library (New York: Doubleday, 1993), 105.

2. My dissertation (STD, Gregorian University, Rome, 1982) was entitled "Christian Community as the Eschatological Family in Lucan Theology." It would be impossible to recount all the sources to whom I am indebted in my study of Luke. However, I would single out the director of my work, Emilio Rasco, SJ, a learned scholar and great mentor. His work on Luke remains for me an important orientation: *La Teologia de Lucas: Origen, Desarrollo, Orientaciones,* Analecta Gregoriana 201 (Roma: Universita Gregoriana, 1976).

3. The Johannine and Petrine models in John have been greatly discussed, recently by Michael H. Crosby, OFM Cap, *"Do You Love Me?" Jesus Questions the Church* (Maryknoll, NY: Orbis, 2000).

4. In recent years, Mary Magdalene has been the topic of much study. The topic is thoroughly studied by Jane Schaberg, *The Resurrection*

of Mary Magdalene: Legends, Apocrypha, and the Christian Testament (New York: Continuum, 2002).

5. Francis J. Moloney, *The Gospel of John*, Sacra Pagina, series editor Daniel J. Harrington, SJ (Collegeville, MN: Liturgical Press, 1998), 360–61.

6. M. Dennis Hamm, SJ, "Ascension" in *The Collegeville Pastoral Dictionary of Biblical Theology*, ed. Carroll Stuhlmueller, CP (Collegeville, MN: Liturgical Press, 1996), 49–52.

7. There has been much discussion recently about science and faith. For background, see Cahal B. Daly, *The Minding of Planet Earth* (Dublin: Veritas, 2004), and Wade Rowland, *Galileo's Mistake: A New Look at the Epic Confrontation between Galileo and the Church* (New York: Arcade, 2001).

8. However, for some observers, there is also evidence of a new Pentecost in Asia in a new, threefold dialogue on culture, religion, and poverty. See Thomas C. Fox, *Pentecost in Asia: A New Way of Being Church* (Maryknoll, NY: Orbis, 2002).

9. Pope Pius XII, Apostolic Constitution, *Munificentissimus Deus* (Defining the Dogma of the Assumption), November 1, 1950.

10. Similar insights are beautifully worked out in the recently published statement "Mary: Grace and Hope in Christ," Anglican–Roman Catholic International Commission (ARCIC), *Origins* 35/3 (2005): 34–50.

11. Pope Pius XII, *Munificentissimus Deus*, §40.

12. Ibid., §39.

13. For a discussion of testamentary form, see Jerome D. Quinn, *The Letter to Titus*, Anchor Bible 35 (New York: Doubleday, 1988), 9, 42–46.

14. The language of this mystery may owe something also to the lived experience of the Middle Ages. The coronation replaced the Last Judgment, which had been the fifteenth mystery in many early listings of the mysteries. The acceptance of the coronation was further involved in a struggle as to whether the prayer should be called the Rosary or the Psalter of the Virgin Mary. To call the prayer a psalter was a way of connecting it with its roots in the imitation of the 150 psalms in the Bible and the use

of a phrase that captures a word in the first verse of each psalm. Later the angelic salutation from Luke would replace the phrase, and then later again, 150 Aves were separated by the Paternosters. Putting the decades in line with meditation on scenes from the life of Christ, aided by artistic renditions, altarpieces, and woodcuts, was a decisive advance. This led to the understanding of the prayer as a garland of roses. Aves were roses offered to Mary, and a crown was made up of five decades of white roses.

The coronation of Mary, although celebrating her glorification in heaven, was imaged as crowning Mary in a rose garden. In many depictions of Mary's coronation, the wall of a rose garden, with intimations of Paradise, was represented by beads. But because of the nuptial and often erotic imagery much beloved in the Middle Ages and frequently attached to garden imagery, some were hesitant to call the prayer a Rosary. Eventually, the name *Rosary* was universally accepted. In this discussion, of course, one will recognize the contemplative need to relate faith to life, interfacing the template of the mysteries of faith with the human need to be enclosed in a garden of love. Many stories that were told to foster the devotion and help build the confraternities that sprang up in many places in Europe explicitly used a rags-to-riches motif. In this way public charity was promoted, although not the full range of social justice as we speak of it today. In one such story, a "charcoaler's daughter" becomes queen. For this story and many more details, see Anne Winston Allen, *Stories of the Rose: The Making of the Rosary in the Middle Ages*, Appendix, 153–60. For a reflection on the Our Father and Hail Mary, see Leonardo Boff, *Praying with Jesus and Mary* (Maryknoll, NY: Orbis, 2005).

15. "Heaven on Their Minds," 1.1, stanza 7, from *Jesus Christ Superstar*, music by Andrew Lloyd Webber, lyrics by Tim Rice (First production, New York: Mark Hellinger Theatre, 1971). Historically, the same accusations of otherworldliness were leveled against the Albigenses, a group in southern France in the thirteenth century whose spirituality rejected life on this earth. It was to confront this heresy that St. Dominic (1170–1221) is said to have preached the praying of the Rosary, according to the legend from the fifteenth century ascribed to Alanus de Rupe

(1428–75), founder of the Confraternity of the Psalter of the Glorious Virgin Mary. Despite these prayers, physical force against the Albigenses was used as well, and was virtually a crusade. This was undoubtedly one of those sins for which John Paul II asked forgiveness in Jubilee Year 2000.

It may be noted in passing that it was between the age of St. Dominic, founder of the Order of Preachers (the Dominicans), and the epoch of Alanus that the Rosary developed through many stages. For our purposes, the most important aspect of the mysteries of the life of Christ is attributed to the Carthusian Dominic of Prussia (1384–1460). Richard Gribble resumes the discussion at the beginning of the twentieth century about this legend. See his introduction and notes in *The History and Devotion of the Rosary* (Huntington, IN: Our Sunday Visitor Publishing Division, 1992), 9–16.

4. THE JOYFUL MYSTERIES

1. Raymond Brown's *The Birth of the Messiah*, the Anchor Bible Reference Library (New York: Doubleday, 1993), is a massive assembly of the scholarship on the infancy narratives, just as his *The Death of the Messiah*, the Anchor Bible Reference Library (New York: Doubleday, 1994), does the same for the passion narrative.

2. While many have written on women's education, there is a new energy in the discussion when development is viewed as freedom. See Amartya Sen, *Development as Freedom* (New York: Anchor Books, 1999). Sen's work can be appreciated from the biblical notion of freedom *from* and freedom *to*.

3. Jerome Murphy-O'Connor, *Paul: A Critical Life* (New York: Oxford University Press, 1998). In this volume Murphy-O'Connor puts together the fruit of his many years of studying Paul. See especially chapters 11 and 12 on Corinth.

4. Peter C. Phan, "Where Are We Going? The Future of Ministry in the United States," *New Theology Review* 18/2 (2005): 5–15. In 2005 the United States Bishops commissioned a study, "Co-workers in the

Vineyard: Resources for the Development of Lay Ecclesial Ministry." There are 30,000 lay ecclesial ministers, full-time and part-time, already working in the United States. See the useful distinctions of ministry and apostolate, secular and sacred, and ordained priesthood versus priesthood of the faithful, in Edward Hahnenberg, "Ordained and Lay Ministry: Restarting the Conversation," *Origins* 35/6 (2005): 94–99.

5. There is a significant use of both the word *reveal* and the word *thoughts* in Romans 1:21 as well, where it is said that the gospel as the power of God, in revealing the wrath of God, discloses the inner struggles of humans. "For though they knew God, they did not honor him as God or give thanks to him but they became futile in their thinking and their senseless minds were darkened." Certainly Paul's remark in Romans takes the issue in the same direction as "inner disarray" but then pushes it much further into darkened minds.

6. At this juncture, a rereading of John Paul's *RVM* may be suggested, especially chapter 1 entitled "Contemplating Christ with Mary." It is commonplace to discuss Mary as a disciple and often with a distinctly feminine hermeneutic. In her work *Whatever Happened to Mary?* (Notre Dame, IN: Ave Maria Press, 2001), Mary Hines cuts to the quick effectively and states all the big issues.

7. Anthony Tambasco, *A Theology of Atonement and Paul's Vision of Christianity* (Collegeville, MN: Liturgical Press, 1991).

8. Although worked out differently, taking these controversies as a whole characterizes also the approach of Luke Timothy Johnson in *The Gospel of Luke*, Sacra Pagina, series editor Daniel J. Harrington, SJ (Collegeville, MN: Liturgical Press, 1991), 317–18.

STUDY GUIDE

INTRODUCTION

1. Is there still a place for popular devotion in the life of the Roman Catholic?
2. Why do you think people have held on to the Rosary?
3. Why did Pope John Paul II add the Mysteries of Light?
4. What does the image of Mary as contemplative add to the Rosary?
5. What is Catholic social teaching, and how does it relate to the claim of the kingdom preached by Jesus?

CHAPTER 1

1. What is it about the role of John the Baptist that seems ever-relevant?
2. What light does the marriage of Cana throw on the story of Jesus?
3. What was Jesus claiming in speaking parables and doing wondrous deeds?
4. What is meant by transfiguration through minor resurrections?
5. Why do we connect the Eucharist to the person of Jesus?

CHAPTER 2

1. From where does the counter-claim to the kingdom come?
2. Does Jesus' suffering resolve the ambiguity of human suffering?
3. How is Pilate's statement "Here is the man" a response to Psalm 8's verse "What is man?"
4. In what way is the way of the cross a journey within a journey?
5. In John's Gospel, what images and details turn the crucifixion into a victory celebration? Explain.

CHAPTER 3

1. If resurrection is not resuscitation to this life, what is it?
2. How does "making captivity captive" explain the ascension?
3. What does Mary know about the Holy Spirit?
4. Is the assumption connected with the communion of saints?
5. Within the contemplation of the Rosary, both Jesus and Mary are crowned. Explain.

CHAPTER 4

1. What aspect of discipleship is presented in both Mary's and Joseph's annunciations?

2. Is the joy of Mary and Elizabeth a gospel value and so to be trusted?
3. Is every birth as significant as Jesus'?
4. Why is Anna's widowhood emphasized by Luke?
5. How is Jesus God's Son?